BOTANIC ACTI
with
David Bellamy

written by

Clare Smallman and David Bellamy

Hutchinson of London
in association with
National Extension College and Thames Television

Contents

Lucky biologists may rush around the world investigating life but there's no reason why you too can't see a little of the action. Get involved in your own environment and explore the way your neighbouring organisms solve their problems. This book is full of ideas ranging from the importance of water to thoughts on taking care of what we've got. On the way you'll find things to make, games to play, experiments to try and some unusual pets. Have fun.

Hutchinson & Co (Publishers) Ltd
3 Fitzroy Square, London W1P 6JD

London Melbourne Sydney Auckland
Wellington Johannesburg and agencies
throughout the world

First published 1978
Text © National Extension College Trust Ltd 1978
Design and illustration © New Leaf 1978

Printed in Great Britain
by Cripplegate Printing Company Ltd, Edenbridge
and bound by Wm Brendon & Son Ltd, Tiptree, Essex

ISBN 0 09 134140 X (cased)
0 09 134141 8 (paper)

Acknowledgements

For Dorothy Dallas
Written by
Clare Smallman and
David Bellamy

Designed at New Leaf,
38 Camden Lock,
Commercial Place,
Chalk Farm Road,
London NW1

by
Michael McGuinness
assisted by
Judith Escreet,
Charles Matheson
Sue Rawkins
and Malcolm Smythe
Drawn by
Safu-Maria Gilbert

Special illustrations
Debbie King,
Michael McGuinness,
Malcolm Smythe
George Thompson
and Ben White

Edited by
Ros Morpeth,
Bob Osborne
and Michael Wright

A special mention
of appreciation to
Malcolm Smythe and
Sue Rawkins without
whom this book may
never have reached
the printer.

Consultant
Michael Feldman,
Associate Producer,
Botanic Man,
Thames Television

Additional research
Martyn Chesworth

Published
in association with
National Extension
College
131 Hills Road
Cambridge
and
Thames Television
306-316
Euston Road
London
NW1 3BB

Build a bottle garden

An enclosed world where water goes round and round

You need

PLANTS:	Small ones in soil
GRAVEL:	From gardener's shop, stream bed or someone's drive (but ask first — and wash the stones)
CHARCOAL:	From an art shop; break into ½ cm (¼ in) bits
GROWING MIX:	Best to buy sterilized potting mixture — either the soil-based or peat-based type from a garden shop
CARDBOARD TUBE:	Narrow enough to go through the neck of your bottle
PLASTIC FUNNEL:	Or a hand-made cardboard one
PLASTIC KNIFE:	
PLASTIC FORK:	
PLASTIC SPOON:	
A NAIL:	
A COTTON REEL:	

WIRE AND SPONGE

FIVE CANES

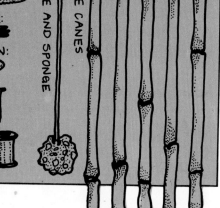

1 Bung (optional)

2 Condensation on top third of inside wall

3 Really clean bottle (use disinfectant and wash well); this is a 10-gallon carboy

4 Plants — small ones! Put the biggest in the middle. Ask the plant seller for advice.

5 Soil mixture 8 cm deep (3″)

6 Charcoal filter 4 cm deep (1½″)

7 Gravel drainage 4 cm deep (1½″)

What to do

MAKE YOUR TOOLS

Push nail into cane to make spine

Make thumper with cotton reel

(glue will help you)

Make spade, fork and cutter from spoon, fork and knife

Wire and sponge

1

Set up funnel and tube. Then put in gravel, then the charcoal and then the soil

Move the tube around the bottle to get the layers even.

2

Use wire and sponge to clean off the sides of the bottle.

DECIDE HOW TO ARRANGE THE PLANTS IN YOUR BOTTLE

3

Dig some holes with your spade.

4

Spike plant root with nail.

5

Lower the plant into position. Use fork to steady plants while thumper is used to firm the soil.

Now plant the other plants

The art of watering

A miniature water cycle

1 Water condenses on the bottle
2 Water runs down bottle.
3 Water soaks into soil.
4 Water enters plant through the roots.
5 Water rises up plant's stem.
6 Water evaporates from leaves and from the bare soil.

P.S. Most plants (except for ferns) like lots of light. But if your sunlight is hot don't put your bottle garden right in it.

How much water does your garden need

For most plants you've got it right if you have condensation on the top third of the bottle. If there's not enough water, spray a little on the leaves. If you overdo it or there's too much condensation to start with, leave the lid off. You are exploiting the way water is re-used in a closed system (which is what you've got). Once the water balance is right you can leave your garden to get on with it.

Other ideas

1 Old fish tank with glass lid planted with orchids.
2 Victorian glass dome from a junk shop. The owl was mouldy and the minature rose is at least alive!
3 Carboy full of ferns. Keep damp and in shade. Fiddly to plant unless you make an extra hole.

Different plants grow in different places. Think of the kind of places they would grow in the wild. And then try and create these conditions in your bottle.

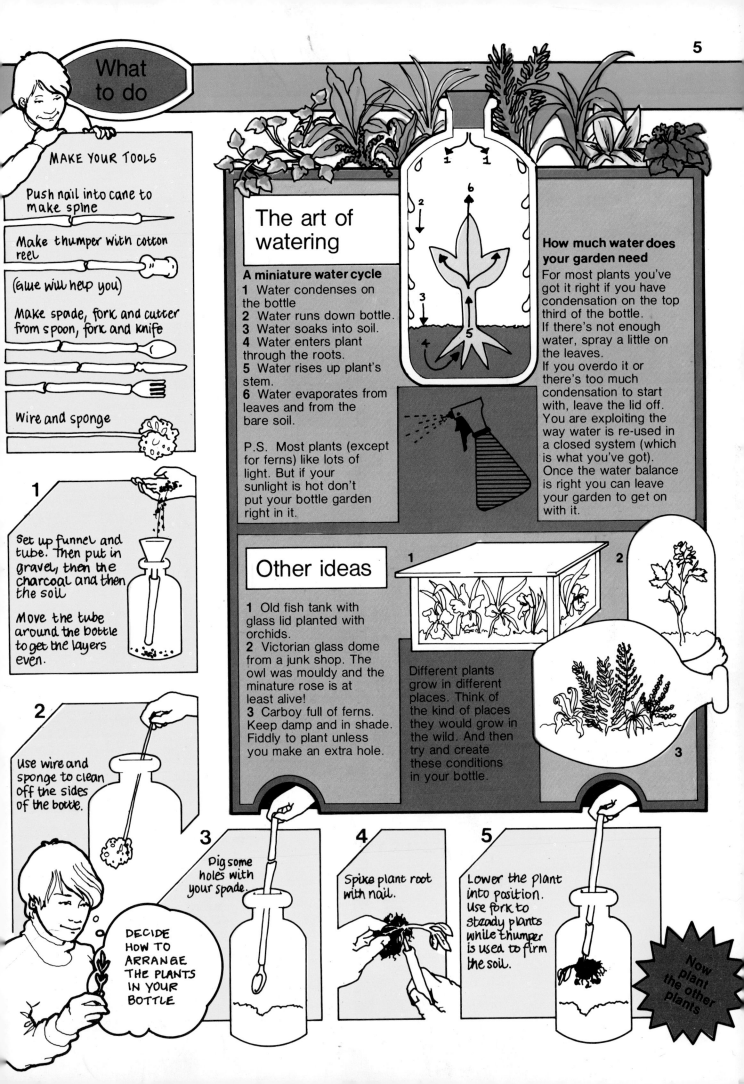

Life without water

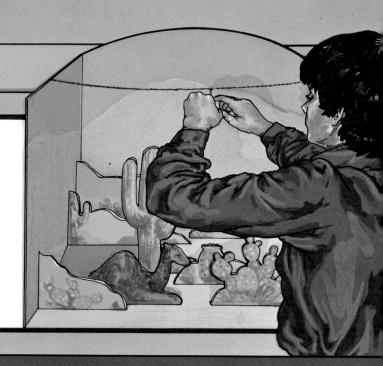

One way of getting a feel for the importance of something like water is to imagine life when it's scarce. 200 million years ago, the whole of Europe, North Africa and much of North America was desert when the land was part of Pangaea (see page 54). Look out of your window and imagine the view as it might have been then — and make yourself a model of the scene. Add some imaginary animals (now long dead, so you can make them up). You may like to have a prowl round your local museum to see what evidence it can provide for the way things were. You are aiming at a three-dimensional scene something like this one.

The framework

YOU WILL NEED: A large rectangular piece of card for the base. A long strip of card for the back and sides. Scissors. Glue and sticky tape (not too narrow). Small pieces of card to act as struts and paints, brushes and fibre tip pens.

What to do

Paint your base a sandy colour all over.

Fold the long strip twice so that you will have two slightly angled side pieces and a curved back.

It should fit on the base like so

View from above

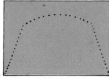

You need a 2cm flap along the bottom of your cardboard strip to stick it to the base. Score a line and fold the flap back. Look out of your window at the far horizon, never mind the bits in between. Imagine it without trees, houses, everything. Draw the horizon line on your background card- quite high up. Colour the sky and paint the hills hazy browns.

Stick background to base. Use card struts for strength.

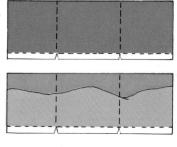

In-between scenery

YOU WILL NEED: The same stuff as before. PLUS:- Fine sand. Some small pebbles. Papier mâché (make sure you ask for old newspapers) or clay — they need to dry hard before you paint them.

What to do

Look at the nearer folds of land- cut out cardboard shapes for the bumps. Each will need a strip along the bottom to glue them to the base.

Foregrounds need to be more detailed.

Put a thin layer of glue over the front few cms of the base. Scatter a thin layer of sand on the glued bits and blow or shake away the excess sand.

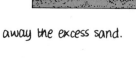

Stick down small pebbles for the close-up rocks. Clay or papier mâché could be used for the nearer hills.

You should now have something that looks like this:

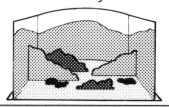

The moment has come to add animals and plants, adapted to live on a low water budget.

The plants

These don't have to look like modern plants, but consider their problems when you design them. They will need to store water, to prevent it evaporating and to protect themselves from animals after their store of water. Here are a few ideas.

Some plants roll up their leaves. You could use slit painted straws which are then stuck into plasticine. Water-losing leaves may be reduced to spines (which give protection too). Stems store water and make food. Use green plasticine and pins or cardboard cut-outs and stick on toothbrush bristles.

Some plants have long water-collecting roots. Make an uprooted plant. Cut it out of paper.

Some plants produce tough seeds to get through drought. Use real seeds in the foreground.

Just after rain, plants are often very exotic. You could show a few in flower. Use paper cut-outs on wire or twisted tissue paper.

The animals

They too want to avoid water loss, grab what water is going and not get too hot. Animals can move into shade or burrows. Birds fly high up where the air is cooler. Plants and animals both have adaptations you can't see very easily — like thick skins and tolerance of temperatures that would kill you. *Moloch horridus* (a lizard) has skin that lets water in but not out. Some adaptations are more obvious.

Show some animals in the shade. Use glass beads as eyes or fluorescent paint and stones.

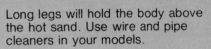

Many animals burrow underground and only come out at night. Paint some animal burrows on the sand.

Some animals have insulating hair on top only. This keeps out heat from the sun. Use painted cotton wool.

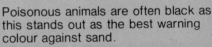

Long legs will hold the body above the hot sand. Use wire and pipe cleaners in your models.

Poisonous animals are often black as this stands out as the best warning colour against sand.

This Tuareg (who lives in the desert) has loose insulating robes.

Extras and alternatives

Add atmosphere with some straggly dark green sponge on distant hills looking like faraway trees and shrub. Also try shadows and a few birds suspended from fine wire. The bigger your model the better. If you've already got a desert outside your window, how about doing a tropical rain forest, or tundra or a scene under a shallow sea? The earth's crust has seen plenty of changes. These photos may give you ideas.

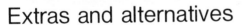

Aqua vita

Water is such a good medium for life that wherever you look, you'll find some organism doing very well thank you. Take Artemia salina, alias the brine shrimp (well why not?), an animal which lives in salty lakes. In some places, water forms pools, dissolves a few salts and evaporates. Before you know it, a puddle salty enough for Artemia has built up. They are found in salt lakes in many parts of the world (but not in the U.K.). In some areas, their water doesn't disappear, it freezes. How does something as small and helpless as Artemia cope? The answer lies in the egg and a very strange way of developing.

A life story

● Egg

Young Artemia starts to develop

If it's too dry, or too cold then the young Artemia goes into state of suspended animation.	If all is warm, wet and generally okay, the young then hatch.

When conditions improve, the egg coating dissolves and the young brine shrimp is triggered into movement by contact with water. It hatches.

The young Artemia is smaller than a pin head. It is a different shape from the adult (e.g. it only has one eye).

You'll see jumps in size over the next few weeks as the little shrimp loses its skin 12 times and does some shape changing. At 25°C it could take three weeks (and good food) to get an adult ½cm long.

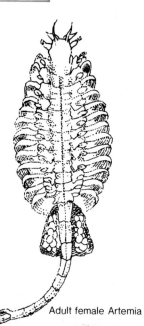
Adult female Artemia

To have your own Artemia collection

You need

A wide necked glass jar

¼ litre of boiled and cooled tap water

AND

EITHER	OR
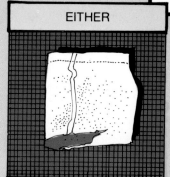	
an all in one salt-and-shrimp pack (look at page 64 for an address to send for these)	brine shrimp eggs from the pet shop (if yours has them) PLUS ½ tablespoonful of non-iodised salt

What to do

1
Tip salt and shrimp eggs into the glass jar.

Add the water.

Keeping them alive

Having hatched your eggs, you have a responsibility. A puddle may not seem much but it's a whole lot more comfy than a glass jar from Artemia's point of view. To successfully breed Artemia, you need to consider food, waste disposal, air and saltiness.

Ripples and a large surface mean that most wild Artemia have plenty of oxygen. Tip your shrimps and water into a new glass jar every few days, and air will dissolve as you pour. Never keep them in a narrow-necked bottle.

Artemia like it salty — but not too salty. Mark the original liquid level and keep your jar topped up to the mark with cooled boiled water. You needn't add salt as only the water evaporates.

Artemia eat single celled organisms. In this case you have to supply a simple food chain. Add, at first, a 1cm square piece of lettuce or cabbage leaf. Bacteria and single celled animals will eat the leaf. Artemia eats the bacteria and minute animals, NOT the leaf, so it's no good adding more leaves. A big leaf will just result in water pollution. Replace the leaf when it's all gone.

Waste won't be a problem unless you added too much leaf. If bacteria multiply faster than they get eaten, the water will go cloudy (a little mist doesn't matter). Usually you can fix things by aerating the contents of your jar. Bacteria aren't very fond of oxygen.

2

Stir. Leave for about 40 hours in a warm place.

3

Watch for the eggs hatching.

A hand lens helps, the babies are very small at this stage.

So does a light behind.

You've got to have soil

Soil profiles

A soil profile is the pattern of layers we find as we go deeper into the ground.

1 A dark mainly organic layer made from decaying animals, plants and their wastes.

2 Lighter organic and inorganic layer. The lower you go the bigger the rocky particles.

3 The parent rock which is what everything sits upon. Sometimes most of layers 1 and 2 have been almost washed away, which makes life difficult. Unless the parent rock is broken down its minerals aren't available for plants. It is difficult to hold on to. Organisms do some of the breakdown, but a lot of it is done by physical forces.

The erosion machine

This machine gives us some idea of nature's sun-powered rock-smashing processes. You might like to design your own machine to do the job. This one is short of animals and plants, but you could include them in your version. Try some of the experiments opposite first for ideas.

Investigate rock smashing forces

Experiment with a model because real rocks take too long to break down and mountains don't fit in the back garden.

You need

A large shallow tray or a seed box

Soil. Stones and gravel

A trowel and watering can (for rain)

Cress seeds

A few unbroken house bricks

A large plastic sheet to work on and somewhere to work (like a backyard)

Maybe an electric fan or hairdryer (wind)

What to do

Fill your box with soil and pack it tightly. This is your model land.

Prop the box up with bricks to make a hillside

Make up some weather – a litre of water makes a monsoon. Are the effects worse if our "land" dries out first? What about wind?

By the time you've cleaned up the mess, you will have some idea of the effect of various physical forces on bare land. The effects of vegetation? – scatter your cress seeds fairly thickly across your 'land'. Let them grow for a couple of days. Try one of the suggestions below.

GRAZING

Be a model cow and harvest half the cress with scissors (for a salad?). Water the box evenly (and energetically). Which has suffered more — the cropped or uncropped? How do both sides rate against bare earth?

TREES AND WIND

Reach for your fan again. Do your model 'trees' reduce the amount of soil that blows away?

TRAMPLING

Animals walk on the vegetation which holds the soil together. See the damage for yourself by trampling your protective vegetation in half the box and watering.

PLOUGHING

This is to try when you've wiped out (or eaten) your cress — plough your field — say with a knife. Do it on a model gentle slope (1 brick) and have half the furrows running across the slope and the other half up and down it. Which results in the land being most affected by rain?

Soil makers and users

Spider

Bristle tail

Mites

Beetle

Ants

Pill millipede

Springtail

Quietly trundling around dead leaves, roots and soil particles are vast numbers of small aquatic animals. Aquatic? In soil? Many animals live in the water held in soil. Their thin skins and fragile constitutions mean that they are imprisoned in their damp world. Expose them to the air and they shrivel and die. Members of the centipedes-as-pets club may be stuck with a dead beast if they forget this. On this page are various ways of investigating the animals that chew and move the most fertile part of soil — the surface layers. Keep them as pets, run races or just look.
P.S. There are lots of organisms too small to see without help, like this nematode worm. If you can lay hands on a microscope, it's well worth looking for them.

Snails

Larva

Pupa

Harvestman

False Scorpion

Centipede

Millipede

Pill bug

Earthworm

Sorting them out

You need

A spade

A sieve

2 plastic washing-up bowls

A funnel

A milk or wine bottle with a little water in it

A fine-mesh hair-net

A shallow dish

A jam-jar with lid and some damp moss in it

A hand lens

What to do

1

Dig up some soil — include some leaf litter. Put it in a washing-up bowl.

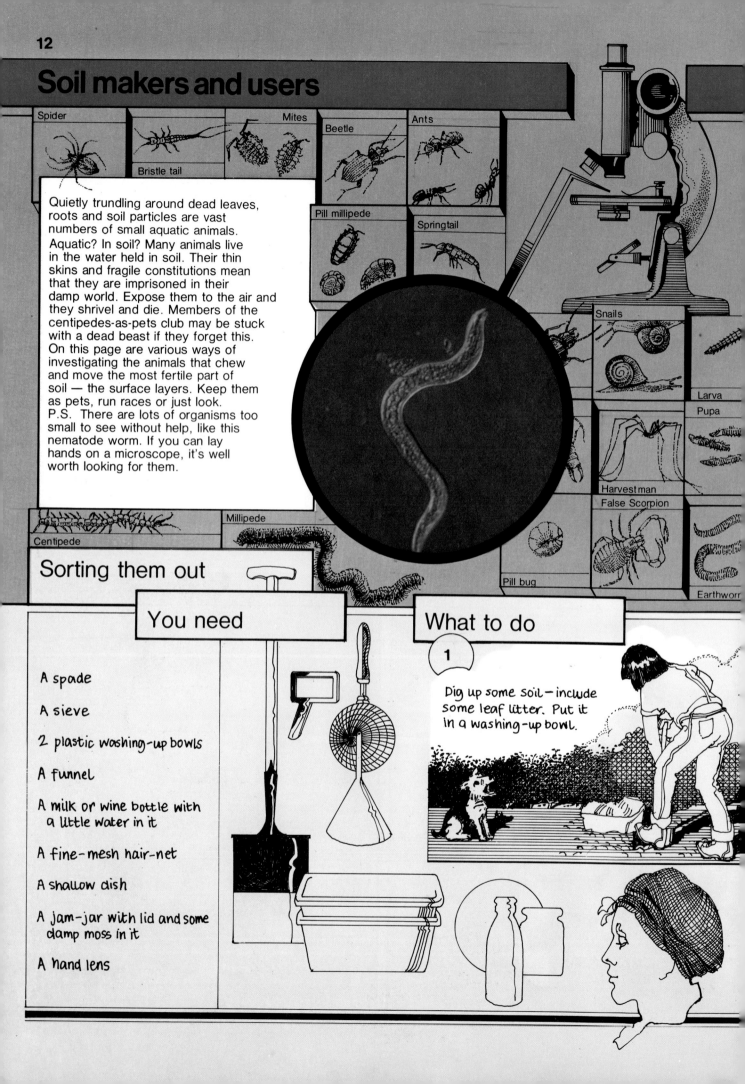

An ant house

Or wormery or whatever. Think about the size of your animals and scale the whole thing up or down as needed.

You need

2 pieces of glass—say 20cm x 10cm

2 pieces of wood—say 20cm x 1cm x 1cm

1 piece of wood—say 10cm x 1cm x 1cm

Wide masking tape
Large stones
Soil and clean sand
Funnel
Piece of clean muslin— 25cm x 15cm

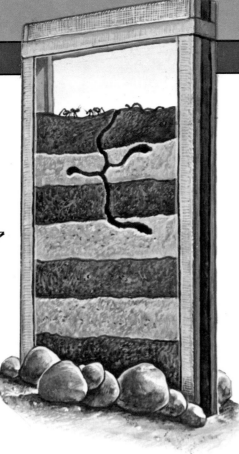

If you want to keep a community with several kinds of animals, a plastic fish tank half full of soil, dead leaves, rotting wood and general dampness (and a lid) will keep them happy (ish).

What to do

Make a wood and glass box—glass sheets held apart with wood.
Tape the whole thing together—tape wrapped round. Stand it up.

Now fill with layers of soil and sand (use a funnel if it gets too messy)—if your animals move soil around, you'll see the sand patterns that result.

Damp, but don't saturate, the soil and don't pack it down too hard.

Put the animals in the top of the box and add some food— you can try leaves, a sugar cube, a bit of raw meat plus anything else you think they might like

Cover the top with muslin and tape it down.

Check it every day or so—keep it damp.

(The big stones on the drawing are to show how the ant house is held upright)

Slug   Earthworm

2

3 Sieved soil goes into the hair-net (or muslin bag).

5 Now sort your entire haul into 4 dishes.

Transfer the soil to the other bowl via the sieve.

Rocks and large animals will stay in the sieve.

Throw away the rocks and dump the animals into the jam-jar for now.

The main groups of invertebrate animals are shown on this page—ask your librarian if you want any more details or information.

4 Lamp (leave it on overnight)

Bag of soil in funnel

Animal falls into bottle in attempt to get away from heat....

What can replace soil?

Imagine a soiless plant

Try making a seedling stand on its root tips. It's not easy because soil provides support as well as water and the mineral salt part of a plant's food. But plants will grow well without soil if you provide these things in other ways. The art is to get the water and mineral balances right while stopping your plants falling over. Here's how to begin.

The support

Start with a container — it can be large or small depending upon whether you want a few tomato plants or a farm! Decide how grand you want to be. Here are some suggestions:

An old tin can will do but will need some holes in the sides and bottom — make these with a nail and hammer. Or you could buy a fair-sized plastic plant pot and saucer.

The ambitious could make a trough with a tray. This can be of wood you nail together yourself. Char the inside by burning a few shavings or small pieces of paper in it until the wood is black — this will stop rot. The trough must have quite a lot of large holes in the bottom. (Or the rich could buy a large plastic window box.)

What to do

1 Put in a thin layer of gravel.

2 Fill to within 1cm of the top of the container with your support material.

3 Top it all off with a thin layer of sand (stabilizing material).

You need

Enough gravel to cover the base for drainage

A trowel

A little sand

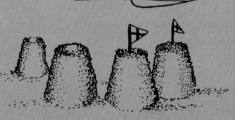

Vermiculite to support your plant. This does not provide any food. Alternatives are lignite, perlite, gravel or sand (in small containers).

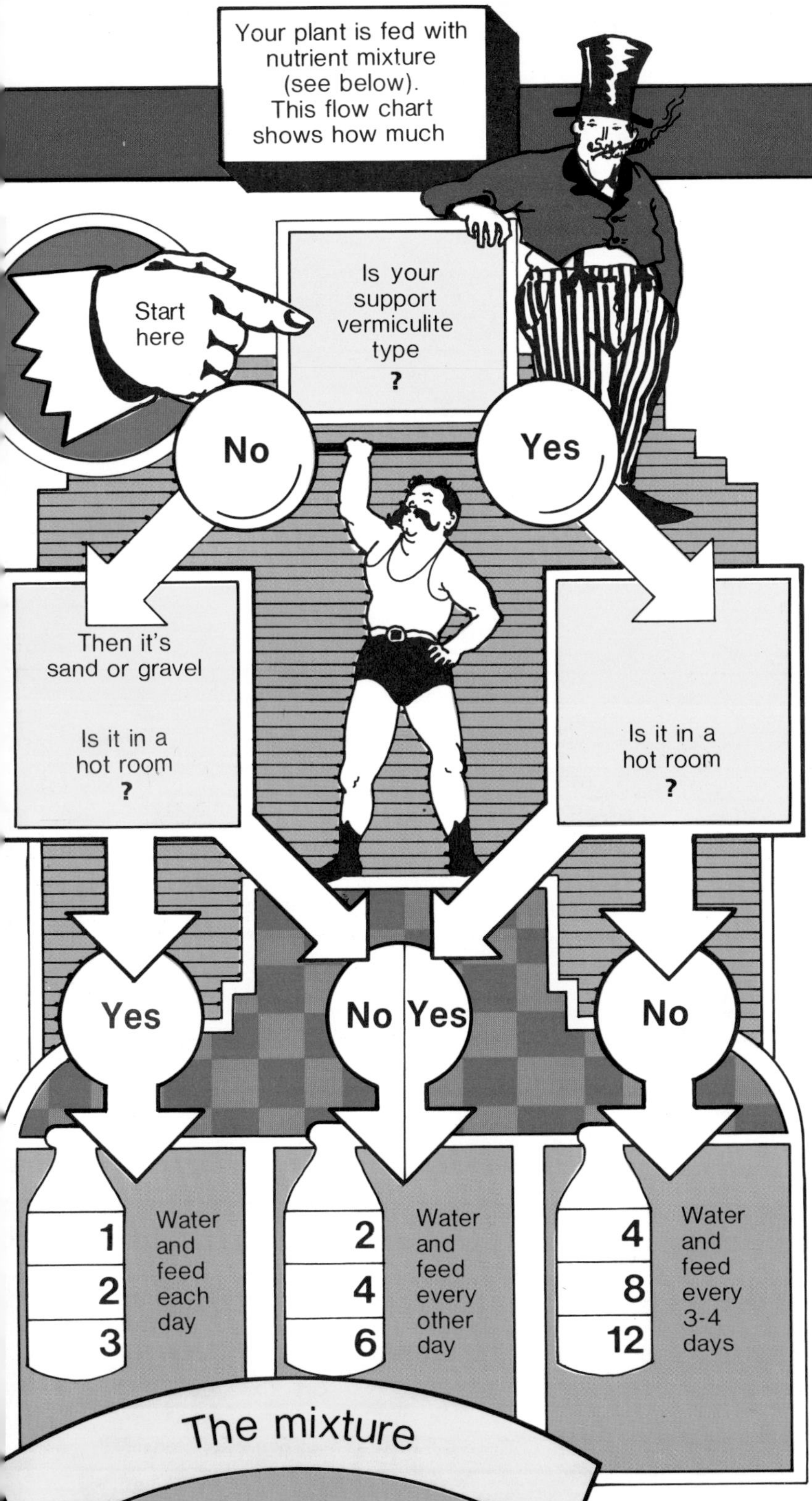

Your plant is fed with nutrient mixture (see below). This flow chart shows how much

Start here

Is your support vermiculite type ?

No

Yes

Then it's sand or gravel

Is it in a hot room ?

Is it in a hot room ?

Yes

No Yes

No

| 1 2 3 | Water and feed each day | 2 4 6 | Water and feed every other day | 4 8 12 | Water and feed every 3-4 days |

The mixture

— water and mineral salts

Plants collect their own carbon dioxide and energy from the environment, but they do need water and a small amount of mineral salts. You have to provide these. The simplest thing to do is to buy a $\frac{1}{2}$ kilogram of prepared salt mixture from a garden shop. Usually $\frac{1}{2}$ a teaspoonful of the salt mixed in a litre container of water is about right. The mixture will keep if you put it in a cool, dark place. Deciding when and how much to water is important. Work through the flow chart (above) to sort out what your plants need. Pour on about $\frac{1}{3}$ of a litre of solution at a time. Every 6 weeks water with plain water to wash your support material.

Planting

First prepare your container of support material by watering with the nutrient solution until it drips through

Make a trench with a pencil

Drop seeds into the trench.

Cover them with ½ cm of sand

Cover the container with a plastic sheet and newspaper until they sprout.

SEEDS

P.S. For the correct time of year and distance apart to sow the seeds, consult the packet they came in.
Seedlings are planted in the same way that you would plant them in soil. Keep everything in a sunny, not too hot place.

Good luck

Tea-time story

Planet Earth may feel big but like the bottle garden, all the materials on it and in it have to be used over and over again. The right mineral salt in the right place is very important. In the tea plantations of Northern India (source of many a cuppa), the monsoon rains now wash the mineral salts down from the hills in enormous quantities. This hasn't always been so — it's only recently that the protecting jungle trees have in places been cleared to grow our tea. The result is that the ground gets less and less fertile.

Tips on using Gro -Kit

Looking around you can often see plants suffering slightly from a shortage of mineral salts. Plants grown without a particular mineral show the effects more clearly. These tomatoes have been grown in 4 types of growing medium. The happy upright specimen of tomatohood has had every nutrient mineral a plant could desire. Deprived of available nitrogen (red bag), phosphorus (yellow bag) or potassium (green bag), the other plants suffer from a variety of ills. Yellowing, purply or shrivelled leaves are all signs that a plant is unable to make some vital substance. All are stunted as a result. Unable to produce seeds they are biological dead ends. There are many other important minerals which become progressively less available to plants if man helps to wash them away. You may like to try this experiment for yourself. The address to send for the Gro-Kit

is at the end of the book. The Gro-Kit contains 4 bags of growing medium, a base board and some capillary matting which acts as a water reservoir. You'll need to keep the matting damp always.
To get water into the bag, cut 2 slits across the bottom of the bag. Also cut a cross in the top.
Push the seeds into the growing medium.
The seeds in the kits

are stock seeds. Hopefully the plant on complete medium will give flowers in 10 weeks. Use a damp matchstick to "plant" them. Try 2 or 3 seeds per bag. Something is bound to germinate. You can pull out the weaker ones leaving one plant per bag.
In winter there is often not enough light for plants to grow as well as they might. Help them along with light-

reflecting aluminium foil around the shaded side of your experimental plot. Stocks need less light than plants like tomatoes in any case. And always keep the matting damp.

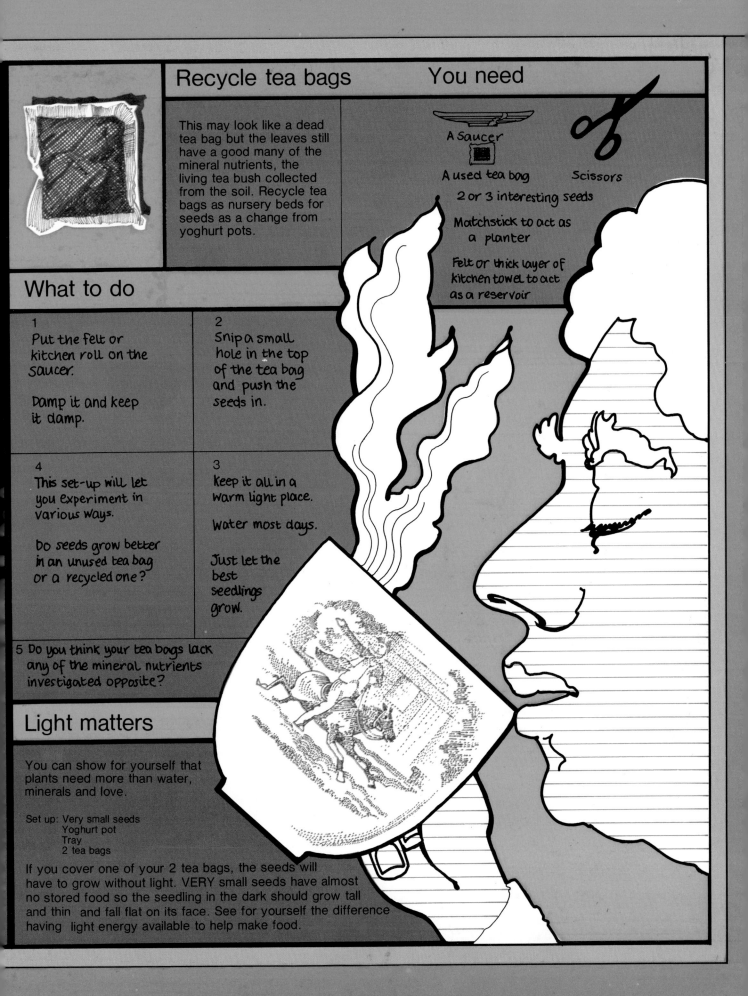

Recycle tea bags

This may look like a dead tea bag but the leaves still have a good many of the mineral nutrients, the living tea bush collected from the soil. Recycle tea bags as nursery beds for seeds as a change from yoghurt pots.

You need

A Saucer

A used tea bag

Scissors

2 or 3 interesting seeds

Matchstick to act as a planter

Felt or thick layer of kitchen towel to act as a reservoir

What to do

1
Put the felt or kitchen roll on the saucer.

Damp it and keep it damp.

2
Snip a small hole in the top of the tea bag and push the seeds in.

4
This set-up will let you experiment in various ways.

Do seeds grow better in an unused tea bag or a recycled one?

3
Keep it all in a warm light place.

Water most days.

Just let the best seedlings grow.

5 Do you think your tea bags lack any of the mineral nutrients investigated opposite?

Light matters

You can show for yourself that plants need more than water, minerals and love.

Set up: Very small seeds
Yoghurt pot
Tray
2 tea bags

If you cover one of your 2 tea bags, the seeds will have to grow without light. VERY small seeds have almost no stored food so the seedling in the dark should grow tall and thin and fall flat on its face. See for yourself the difference having light energy available to help make food.

Animals rot...

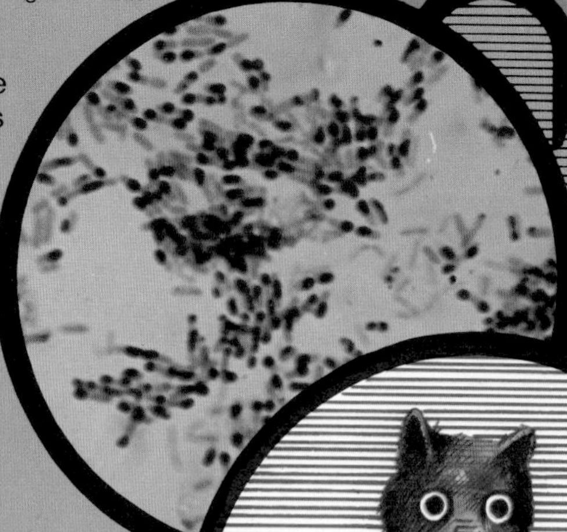

Bacteria from woodland soil enlarged 5,000 times — the kind of organism that decomposes dead organic matter

Micro-organisms like these, with a little help from their friends, quickly reduce a dead mouse to a few bones and the few bones to chemicals for re-use by others. Halt the process of decay by cleaning and drying the skeleton and you'll have the start of a fascinating collection. Scraping the flesh off bones is not very pleasant. Happily, there are lots of natural recycling processes to do it for you. Owls can help or you could use scavengers if you can trap them.

Trapping scavengers

Faced with a dead mouse or similar offering from your cat you could bury it near the surface of a box of damp soil. Micro-organisms in the soil will pare the body to the bone in a few weeks. Always wear rubber gloves to handle dead animals or use tongs or a trowel to carry them. They are usually crawling with ticks which can carry human diseases. Your decomposing box is best out of doors away from the house. You can speed things up by adding some of the larger scavengers which help the micro-organisms. To trap them . . . .

You need

A trowel

A little chopped meat

A large yoghurt pot or jam-jar

4 small stones

A bit of wood (15cm x 15cm)

What to do

Dig a pit deeper than your pot. Sink the pot into it.

Bait your trap — with small pieces of meat.

Balance the wooden lid on the 4 stones. This is to prevent flooding and to provide shade. Leave for a day or two.

Tip your collection of visitors into your decomposing box, and put on a lid.

Let owls do the work

You could take advantage of the fact that digestion breaks up flesh. Birds like owls swallow their prey whole. Their digestive juices dissolve the flesh and they throw up pellets containing only bones and fur.

An owl pellet.

1 Owl pellet
2 Soak owl pellet in water (for an hour or so).
3 Tweezers and pins.
4 Take pellet to pieces in shallow dish.

You'll find them:
— under owls' nests in barns
— in old fireplaces in deserted houses
— under isolated trees and posts

5 Bleach bones in dilute hydrogen peroxide. Use this trick on all bones you collect. Leave them in for a few minutes only.
6 Wash in water.
7 Dry the clean bones.

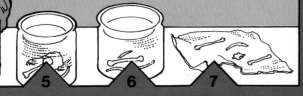

Mounting skeletons

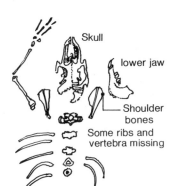

Skull
lower jaw
Shoulder bones
Some ribs and vertebra missing

Hip bones
Vertebrae
Rabbit skull

Not all the bones are present — small ones often go astray or fall apart

Small mammal skeletons look good mounted on card. Try arranging them to show how they fit together - if you find the bits confusing you can borrow a book or feel your own bones as a guide.

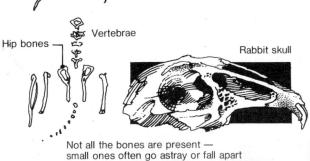

This upturned shell was once the home of an Aldabra tortoise. Local scavengers have picked the bones clean.

...Plants decay

A dead land plant breaks down in two stages. The soft parts decay and are used, quite quickly, by other plants as they grow. The leaf skeleton is tougher — after all it holds the plant up, and it takes much longer to rot. If you catch it in time you can try some of the ideas opposite.

Seaweeds are supported by water and are soft all the way through. They decay fast — as you'll discover if you collect some to make prints and forget them for a day or so! Don't rip them off the rocks — use loose ones.

This is a Victorian pressed seaweed. They got really hooked on making collections, and you can see why. Seaweeds have done very well for themselves in the sea. You may be surprised how many kinds you find.

Leaf skeletons the slow but natural way

Cheating with leaf skeletons

You need

11 tablespoons (150 gm) sodium carbonate (Na_2CO_3)

10 tablespoons (136 gm) slaked lime ($Ca(OH)_2$)

both from a chemist (drug store)

Measuring jug and basin

A spoon

Tweezers

Two saucers

A sieve and second-best saucepan

WARNING

The aim is to dissolve leaves not your fingers. If you slop any of the solutions over yourself, wash it off with lots of water. At once!

Pressing seaweed

You need

A largish sheet of white paper and a dish large enough for it to fit into

Paint-brush, scissors and muslin

Drying papers (1 sheet of blotting paper and 3 sheets of newspaper)

3 or 4 fairly heavy books

A board to put everything on and, of course, some seaweed

What to do

1 Submerge the paper in the dish of water

2 Float the weed above the paper. Snip off the bushy bits and arrange the weed with a paint brush.

Ponds and streams are full of creatures partial to soft leaves. If you're short of water for collecting animals, hatch out some fresh water shrimps (you can buy eggs at a pet shop) and let them loose on a leaf. One leaf per jar is plenty — otherwise you'll end up with a nasty soup.

Pencil
Thread
Jar
Unfortunate leaf
Hungry fresh-water shrimps
Use pond, stream or rain barrel water

What to do

1 5 odium carbonate — 500 ccs of water

2 Add slaked lime and boil for 15 minutes

3 Sieve liquid into bowl

CHIEF SCIENTIST   TEMPORARY LAB. ASSISTANT
* Rather important is a lab coat (alias an apron)

4 The stuff you want is in the basin, not the sieve

5 Pour the liquid back into the pan

6 Add the leaves and boil for one hour

7 Use tweezers to remove leaf skeletons

8 Wash gently. Fine veins are very fragile

9 Dry flat and use

Uses for leaf skeletons

MAKE A COLLECTION

Useful book on trees
Labels
Glue
Leaf skeleton

OR USE THEM AS PICTURES

These leaf skeletons were painted and allowed to dry before being stuck down.

OR MAKE LEAF PRINTS

Newspaper
Card
Leaf — painted side up
Newspaper

Put wet leaf into this 'sandwich'.

Paint skeleton gold (or whatever).

Then roll it gently and evenly. Peel off the layers.

3 Lift the paper and weed carefully.

Tip them a little to drain and put them on the board.

4 Pile on as follows:

muslin,
then blotting paper,
then newspaper
and finally the books

5 Change the drying papers daily. Allow about a week before revealing your pressed weed.

The food chain game

4 Top carnivores eat intermediate carnivores

3 Intermediate carnivores eat herbivores

Adult trout

2 Herbivores eat plants.

Caterpillar

Land snail

1 Plants use sun energy and soil mineral salts (among other things) to grow.

Moss

Grass

Nettle

5 Animals and plants eventually die. Decomposers break down dead animals and plant material to salts that plants can use.

Mineral salt also START

P.S. Carnivores eat meat. You are an omnivore because you can eat everything.

The rules

1
Four people are about the most that can play. Everyone has two counters. Start at the mineral salt level. The aim is to get both counters at once to the top carnivore level (and to stop other people from getting there).Counters are moved separately. You will also need a dice with a sun symbol on

the odd numbers (see p.62).

2
You must throw a sun symbol to start as plants need energy to use the mineral salts. Numbers don't matter here. Choose any plant to move to.

3
To get to the next link in the

chain, you simply move your counter ahead when it is your turn. You don't need the dice for this. You move one link at a time. If you choose to throw a dice to start a counter, you can't then change to a move further up the chain. You must move to something that is likely to eat the organism you are sitting on — e.g. from wheat to

Heron

Owl

Man

Tit mouse

Pike

Spider

Cyclops

Predatory beetle

Frog

Thrush

Daphnia

Mouse

Water snail

Leaf-eating fly

Small fish

Oak tree

Algae

Wheat

Algae

Water weed

"On Ilkley Moor baht 'At" is an old song about a food chain. The relevant words are on the right. Can you spot the missing link?

Weer has tha bin sin a sor tree?
On Ilkley Moor baht 'At
Av bin a coortin' Mary Jane
On Ilkley Moor baht 'At
Then thee'll catch tha death o' cowd
On Ilkley Moor baht 'At
Then we shall have to bury thee
baht 'At
cum an' eat thee up
baht 'At
cum an' eat up worms
baht 'At
cum an eat up ducks
baht 'At

...ouse. (Sometimes this means ...ou can miss out a level.) If ... doubt, there is a check list ...f what eats what on page ...2 — you can use it as ...vidence if you think ...omeone has made a ...istake. If you make a false ...ove you must die and be ...ecomposed to a mineral ...alt.

4
You can stop your opponents by challenging them for the organism they are on, but only if it's on your route — e.g. if they are on a spider and you are on a fly. If it is plausible, challenge sideways, e.g. a spider could be eaten by a frog. Opponents throw the dice — the higher number survives,

the other dies and is decomposed.

5
Once dead you must be treated by decomposers — like earthworms and bacteria. Move your piece into the mineral salt area and wait to spin a burst of energy in order to start up the chain again.

You and food chains

You are the last link in many food chains. There are two types. One is a biological food chain. You eat animals who eat plants though you also eat greenery direct. The other food chain involves transporting food to you. Research both types of chain.

The true food chain

The food you eat needed a certain amount of room to grow. Even if you are eating meat, the cow or chicken or fish ate plants which needed a place to grow. As a result you live off a much larger chunk of the earth's surface than the bits you walk on and are used to seeing. You are a space consuming animal. Compare the area needed to grow your usual diet with that needed for a meat-free day (meatless part on the next page).

What to do

You need to choose a unit to measure the amount you eat. It could be a spoonful, a forkful or a cupful. The big thing is to be consistent. You'll have to do a bit of guessing.

Write down each food as you eat it (and don't forget all the liquids).
Write down how much you eat of each food in your chosen unit in the table.
Look up your score. Award yourself:
1 spacepoint for each unit of plant material (lettuce, bread, tea etc.)
5 points for each milk and eggs unit
10 points per unit for all other animal foods. And this is being kind!

Personal daily space needs			
	What you ate	How much (in same units)	Space score
Breakfast			
Midday meal			
Evening meal			
Snacks			
			Total

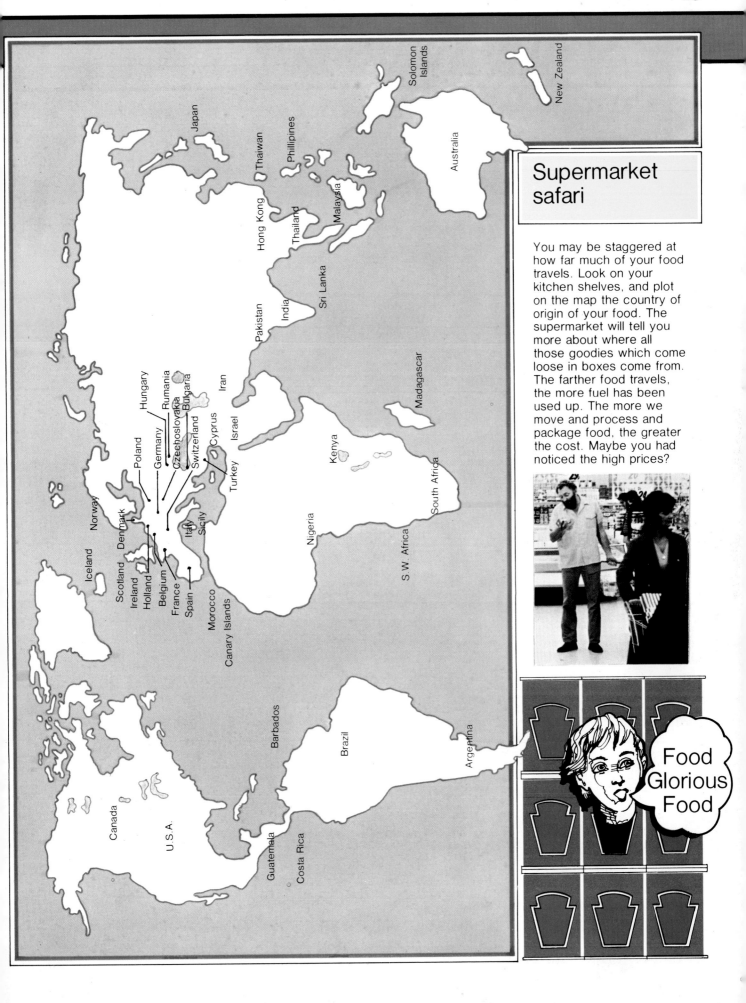

Supermarket safari

You may be staggered at how far much of your food travels. Look on your kitchen shelves, and plot on the map the country of origin of your food. The supermarket will tell you more about where all those goodies which come loose in boxes come from. The farther food travels, the more fuel has been used up. The more we move and process and package food, the greater the cost. Maybe you had noticed the high prices?

Food Glorious Food

Eat low in your food chain

Eating low in your food chain basically means doing without meat. Stagger your family with a meat-free meal and see what happens to the space needed to grow your food. Fill in the chart as on the previous page.

Meal	What you ate	How much you ate	Space units
Breakfast			
Midday meal			
Evening meal			
		Total	

Vegetable biryani

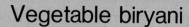

You need

1 tablespoon of butter

Big pinches of cayenne pepper (if you have any), turmeric and ground ginger

½ teaspoon each of cumin and mustard seeds

¼ teaspoon each of salt, cinnamon and coriander

Bunch of chopped salad onions

100 gms each of yellow wax beans, cooked long-grain rice and saffron rice

1 large red pepper — seeded and chopped, and the same of aubergine (egg plant)

2 tablespoons of cashews and raisins

The great thing to remember about a biryani is that if you haven't got exactly what the recipe says, you can sling in any vegetables you fancy, such as mushrooms and peas, as long as you chop the big ones up. The spices are fairly important — this recipe will give you a mild dish with enough for four people.

What to do

Melt the butter in a big pan

Add all the spices and stir for a couple of minutes

Add all the vegetables — and keep stirring

When in doubt, undercook. You are aiming at soft, but not mushy vegetables. Remember the veg. will go on cooking in the oven.

Fill the casserole or glass baking dish with a layer of white rice, the vegetables and beans, and the yellow saffron rice, in that order.

Top off with the nuts and raisins.

Cover and cook at 325°F (gas mark 3) for 40 minutes

A Mexican snack

You need

4 tablespoons vegetable oil

1 tablespoon chopped onion

½ cup tomato purée

2 cups beans – kidney or Mexican or whatever

A little chilli powder – optional, but worth it

Salt

Sieve, pan, bowls, frying pan, spoon and fork

What to do

Soak the beans overnight

Cook them in 5 cups of water quite gently until soft – it takes about 2 hours in a covered pan

Drain, but KEEP THE LIQUID

Fry the beans for 10 minutes. Use half the oil. Mash them.

Add the cooking liquid a little at a time – stir gently as you add and the beans will absorb the water.

Fry the onions in the remaining fat until they are semi-transparent

Add the tomato purée and chillis and stir, then stir-in the beans. Eat it all very hot.

You need

Courgette surprise

250 gms of soya-bean and ¼ litre of the liquid the beans were cooked in

2 big courgettes (or a small marrow)

3 tablespoons of butter

½ tablespoon of thyme
1 tablespoon of parsley
(Fresh if you can get it)

2 crushed garlic cloves

1 chopped onion

½ teaspoon of dill or coriander

Pepper

3 tomatoes and 80 gms of parmesan cheese

What to do

Wash the beans and soak them overnight in salted water

Cook for 3 or 4 hours until beans are tender. You can add water as you go along. You will need ¼ litre left at the end

Melt the butter in the pan and fry the onions and garlic until they are tender.

Add all the herbs. Are you stirring? Cook for 2-3 minutes

Add the beans and the cooking liquid and simmer for ¼ hr.

Grease a large casserole or oven-proof dish

Chop up the courgettes and tomatoes

Add cheese to bean mix and stir the whole lot well

Put half of everything in the dish in layers — beans followed by tomatoes, then courgettes

You should be able to repeat the layers as above

Decorate with freshly ground pepper and butter dabs

Bake for 3 hours at 300°F (gas mark 2) and serve it hot with green salad — you'll amaze everyone!

What's it all about?

Probably you had a much lower space score on your meat-free day. Here's why.

When plants grow, they need space (for light and water and so on). Pretend it takes 1 sq. metre of land to grow the wheat to make a loaf.

Suppose you want to have the same amount of food, but as meat, Chickens turn plant material into meat for us. Unfortunately they don't do it very efficiently — in fact now we need 10 sq. metres of wheat.

Look back at the food chain game. The more links in the chain, the more enormous the losses. Draw for yourself a diagram of a person eating a fish which has eaten a little fish which has eaten water plants. Put in the losses. Perhaps we'll eat bread instead — would we need (a) $\frac{1}{10}$th, (b) $\frac{1}{50}$th, (c) $\frac{1}{100}$th the amount of plant material used up in the fish dinner? Does it matter? Decide for yourself.

The energy game

Imagine you are a plant. Being alive, you need energy to grow and reproduce and survive the various disasters on the way to the finish. You collect energy for this from the sun. The amount of energy you have is measured in points, and you start with 100 points in your account. Think of energy as money — don't overdraw and you'll be OK. You'll need two counters per player and a dice. The rules go like this:

1 Everyone has one counter to act as a marker. Start with it on the 100 line. Move it down the scale as you use up energy. If your account gets low you can collect energy from the sun. To do this, throw the dice, but instead of moving add ten times the dice score to your energy account. If you run right out of energy, you have to start again.

2 Everyone has a second counter at the start. Move it forward by the number you throw. Moving uses energy, so lose 10 points from your account for every move. You will meet many crises on the way to the finish which will also cost you energy points from your account.

3 Some squares give you the option to invest in a seed (for the price of a few energy points). Should you get eaten later on, return to your seed investment instead of starting again.

4 The winner is the one that makes it to the finish first with something left in the energy account.

START

Aphid sucks your sap — lose 5 points

Damaged twig to repair — lose 10 points

Grow a flower which is wrecked by rain — lose 10 points

Nice sunny day — add 10 points

You can choose to invest in a seed — it'll cost you 15 points

Another plant has grown very fast and is now shading you — lose 5 points

Eaten down to your roots but you cope; whoops — lose 25 points

A leaf or two gets eaten — lose 5 points

Glorious growing weather — add 10 points

No sun for days — lose 5 points

Very hot day. You wilt — lose 10 points

Plant entirely eaten — go back to start

Opportunity to invest in a seed — it'll cost you 15 points

Dry weather — lose 5 points as your roots grow in search of water

Roots eaten by wire worms — lose 10 points in repairing

Humans pick most of you — lose 15 points for repairs

Opportunity to invest in a seed — it'll cost you 15 points

Too hot a day — lose 5 points to repair damage

Plant entirely eaten — back to start

Stormy night; half your shoot breaks off — lose 15 points

FINISH

ENERGY BANK ACCOUNT
100
95
90
85
80
75
70
65
60
55
50
45
40
35
30
25
20
15
10
5
0
OUT

Feeling energetic?

We get our energy from food — carbohydrates which plants have made using sun energy. Investigate the effects on your body chemistry of the energy tied up in these chemical packages.

What to do

1 Measure your own pulse rate — count the thumps over one minute and write the number down. (this is important for later comparison). If you can't find a pulse at your wrist, try feeling under your jaw. Everyone has their own normal pulse rate. Now carry out some fairly violent exercise, like running on the spot for, say, two minutes.

2 Take your pulse again. Keep doing it until it is back to your pre-exercise level.

3 Now you have an idea of your recovery time. Repeat the whole thing having sucked a glucose tablet. Give yourself long rests between the tests — perhaps even doing them on different days. Try out other foods such as chocolate.

A

Your weight in kilogrammes:

(a) Activity	(b) Energy need in kilocals/ kg/min	(c) Your energy needs in kilocals/min (multiply figures in (b) by your weight in kg)
Swimming Fast bicycling Lots of exercise	0.14	
Gentle bicycling Rapid carpentry	0.04	
Writing Sitting Sewing Reading aloud	0.0065	
Washing up Rapid typing Floor cleaning Driving Light exercise	0.016	
Dressing Singing loudly	0.011	
Walking Skating Moderate exercise	0.06	
Rowing in a race Boxing match	0.2	

How much energy do you need?

The kilocalorie or Calorie is the amount of energy needed to raise the temperature of a litre of water by 1°C. Not easy to imagine, alas, but we measure our energy input and output in kilocalories nevertheless! If you want to work out your energy needs for half an hour, enrol a friend with a watch and pencil, thrust this book into their hands and tell them to fill in the first two columns in table B below. Then use table A left to fill in your energy needs. For activities not mentioned, give yourself the score of the most similar form of exercise on the table. Slimming books love tables of food energy content so you can work out if your diet gives you too much or too little energy.

B

Activity	Doing time in minutes	Energy needed in kilocals
	Total energy needed	

Where does our energy come from?

Your energy-rich glucose was made by a plant which could trap the energy in sunlight. There is a great deal of energy still tied up in rotting plants — think about coal. For more current evidence, take a poke at your nearest stagnant pond.

Coal formation takes time

It also takes heat and pressure. There is no point in investing in swamps in the hope that you will get coal in your lifetime! Fossil fuels are the results of millions of years of energy collection. Get-rich-quick types should contemplate the time-scale — coal is older than the Alps and Rockies put together. It was formed before the supercontinent of Pangaea (see page 54) broke up.

You need

A good friend to pull you out....

A stagnant pond

Half a sawn-off washing up liquid container tied onto a forked branch (optional).

Rubber boots

Some long sticks

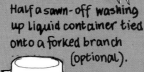

A cigarette lighter or matches (but **BE VERY CAREFUL**. It's all too easy to burn down a forest. If there are many trees around, skip the flame bit)

What to do

①

Give your stagnant pond a good poke. Unspeakable pongy gasses will bubble up.
These are some of the results of plants decomposing in stagnant (no oxygen) water.
They include hydrogen sulphide and methane.

You may at this point give up.

②

The energy tied up in methane can be used as a fuel. When lit, it will burn with a pale blue light which is easiest to see on dull days. You can try lighting a bubble with a rush torch — but only if all around you is sodden.

RUSH TORCH:
A bundle of dry grass wedged into a forked stick like this.

You can collect the gas in your upturned container if you have any trouble getting at it.

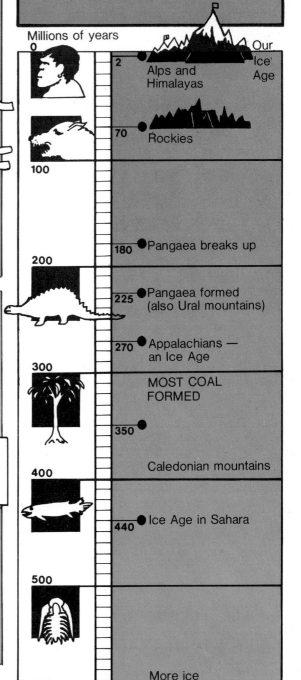

Millions of years

0	
2 ●	Alps and Himalayas — Our Ice Age
70 ●	Rockies
100	
180 ●	Pangaea breaks up
200	
225 ●	Pangaea formed (also Ural mountains)
270 ●	Appalachians — an Ice Age
300	MOST COAL FORMED
350 ●	
400	Caledonian mountains
440 ●	Ice Age in Sahara
500	
600	More ice

Weeds as winners

Weeds are plants which are highly successful in places where man doesn't want them. Gazing out of your window at dandelions and rosebay willow herbs that are doing well despite you may cause you to despair — or wonder. Try to work out how the situation has arisen. Start by watching to see which animals eat them. Many plants become pests when they are not being eaten fast enough. Perhaps an enthusiast with an insecticide spray has killed off hungry insects. Or the weed may grow amazingly fast. You can investigate this too.

Water hyacinth *left* is a weed to people in India because none of the local animals will eat it. Back home in South America it's kept in check by hordes of water hyacinth eaters.

Rosebay willow herb

Dandelion

Growing bits of plants

This method of growing bits of plants usually works. Use it for the investigations on the next page.

What to do

1
Label your pots to avoid any muddles — write on the labels the contents and where they came from and the date

2
Half-fill the pot with moist compost (about as damp as a wrung-out sponge)

3
Put in one bit of plant. Cover it with about 1cm of compost.

4
Cover pots with plastic for two days or so. Let things grow (or not!) for a week and note the results you get

5
Start thinking about transplanting to pots if you want to grow them further.

You need

Lots of yoghurt pots. Soil or, better still, potting compost. Labels. Cling-film or plastic bags. Interesting chunks of plants.

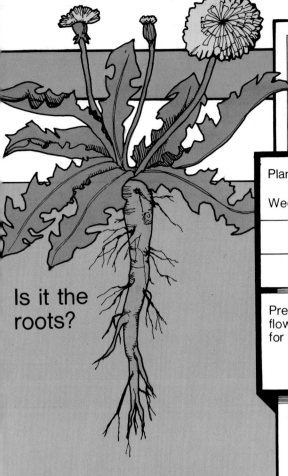

Is it the roots?

Maybe weeds have particularly tough and resilient roots. Dig up a few of your most hated weeds plus a few garden flowers for comparison.
Chop up the roots and try growing the bits. Which sprout best — weeds or flower roots? Which is harder to dig up completely — a dandelion or a tulip?

Dig up a whole lot of dandelion roots
Chop them up
Dry them in air overnight
Roast them in the oven for one hour
Grind them up

Now use them as coffee substitute.
(Well, this isn't all science.)

You could experiment with roasting other roots, like carrots, and adding them to the mixture.

Flowers as secret weapons

One way of dealing with harassment if you are a plant is to be very prolific (reproduce a lot). Investigate by doing some counting. Draw your own table and give yourself lots of room. Do more than one count — you may have an odd plant.

Plant group	Name	Flowers per plant				Or seeds per flower			
		1	2	3	4	1	2	3	4
Weeds	e.g. Dandelion	2	4	4	3	48	31	28	37
Pretty garden flower plants for comparison									

Will you be pulling weeds up before or after they flower in future? Putting them on the compost heap will just result in a great weed patch. How about pressing them instead? Weed flowers may be small but lots on a bookmark look great.

What to do

1. Make a sandwich of your flowers between sheets of blotting paper

2. Surround it with two or three sheets of newspaper

3. Put the whole thing under three heavy books (wonderful things telephone directories)

4. Leave for a couple of weeks

5. Mount the flowers on card and hold in place and cover at the same time with clear plastic film

Perhaps they just grow fast

You will need some weed seeds (and some garden flower seeds for comparison). Let them grow in pots — several of each kind. Which germinated (sprouted) first?
Put them out in your garden in their pots. Which has grown most at the end of the two weeks? There are various ways of keeping track of growth. An easy one is to measure how tall they have grown. Mind you, it's hardly fair to compare naturally short plants with ones that usually grow quite tall. Allow for that in your choice of seeds for the experiment. A rapid start means that a plant has first grab at space, light and water. It also means seeds are produced more quickly. How did your weeds rate in the race for life? Moral: he who goes on holiday and leaves his weeds to their own devices deserves what he gets.

Support your local weed

Close-up of a
nettle sting

Weeds cope very well with humans and other pests.
A nettle's stinging hairs are an attempt to reduce the
chance of being eaten. We adapt to them with gloves or by
destroying them. But a nettle
patch in a quiet corner
can be fun. Here
are some ideas:

Peacock
caterpillar

Red admiral

Nettle Brotchen [BROTH]

What to do

Wash the nettles – keep your gloves on

Chop them into ½-leaf sized bits

Add oat meal to boiling milk and
butter mix and stir a bit

Add nettles and salt and pepper

Put the lid on let it simmer
for 45 minutes

Sling in the parsley and boil
it for 2 or 3 minutes

serve – a splash of cream
improves it no end!

You need

2 cups of young nettle tops –
packed tight

knob of butter

tablespoon of chopped parsley

tablespoon of flakey oatmeal

1 pint of milk

pinch of salt and pepper

Nettlepower in the garden: keep a
handful of nettles in a bucket of
water (outside!) for 5 days. Splash
the liquid around your plant roots.
Aphids leave your plant in hordes.

Nettles as a natural hair rinse:
boil 1 cup of nettles with 3 cups
of water. Strain and cool. Rub it
into your hair after shampooing.

1
Store your nettles in the bucket until they start to rot. Keep them well away from the house... phew!

Nettle paper

Nettles have a supporting fibre skeleton. These tough fibres can be used to make paper.

You need

lots of whole nettle plants

a fairly unloved pan (large) and spoon

a bucket

bleach *

caustic soda *

> **WARNING!**
> * You can damage yourself with this - wash off any splashes at once.

big washing-up basin and large piece of rag

big scissors or shears

pestle and mortar or electric blender

2 blankets or something equally thick and absorbent

a wooden frame with a bit of perforated zinc tacked to it. Make it yourself from 5 nails and 5 bits of wood.

tongs and a large tough apron

More weeds to love

Bindweeds are a plague, but you can make use of their stems as free plant ties — after all they have specialized in being long, tough and flexible. Some weeds have scented leaves which make splendid bookmarks when pressed. There is also an excellent game called plantain bashing. It is great for getting rid of small kids when you're supposed to entertain them and you have better things to do. Opponents find themselves champion plantain flowerheads and take turns at trying to decapitate the opposition's weapons. I have always regretted getting strong enough to do the job in one go. Maybe with a tougher weed . . .

2
Tip them into the basin. Fill the bucket with bleach and make up a caustic soda solution in the pan. (One cup of crystals to a pan ¾ full of water.)

Boil the rotting leaves in caustic soda a few at a time. Prod them around a bit. Rinse away the soft squelchy parts. Then put the remaining fibres into the bleach.

3
When they go straw coloured, wash the fibres and wrap them in the rag. Wring them dry.

4
Chop them up and then grind the pieces to pulp.

5
Put the pulp in warm water in the basin. Spread it out and then scoop it up with your zinc paddle sieve.

Let it drain.

6
Turn it out onto a damp blanket. Put a blanket on top and weigh the whole lot down with some heavy books.
Leave it overnight.

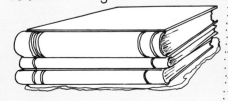

Release your sheet and dry it out finally.

Admire it and use it.

Spider-sized problems

Organisms can adapt to problems presented by their environment by changing their behaviour.
Spiders are pretty brainless, but they can alter their daily routine when faced with an emergency. If the disaster isn't too unlikely, they can react constructively. You can investigate their ability to adapt with help from your friendly local web-spinning spider. This is *Araneus*. Search for its superb even orb webs in gardens. You may find other web-spinners in the process.

Common garden spider (*Araneus diadematus*)

This web has been magnified by 1000 times and on this scale the spider would be bigger than a bus. The threads are immensely strong, and will hold a writhing moth or an angry insect larger than the spider itself. Even so, breaks happen and webs disintegrate. How do spiders adapt their behaviour to cope with these disasters?

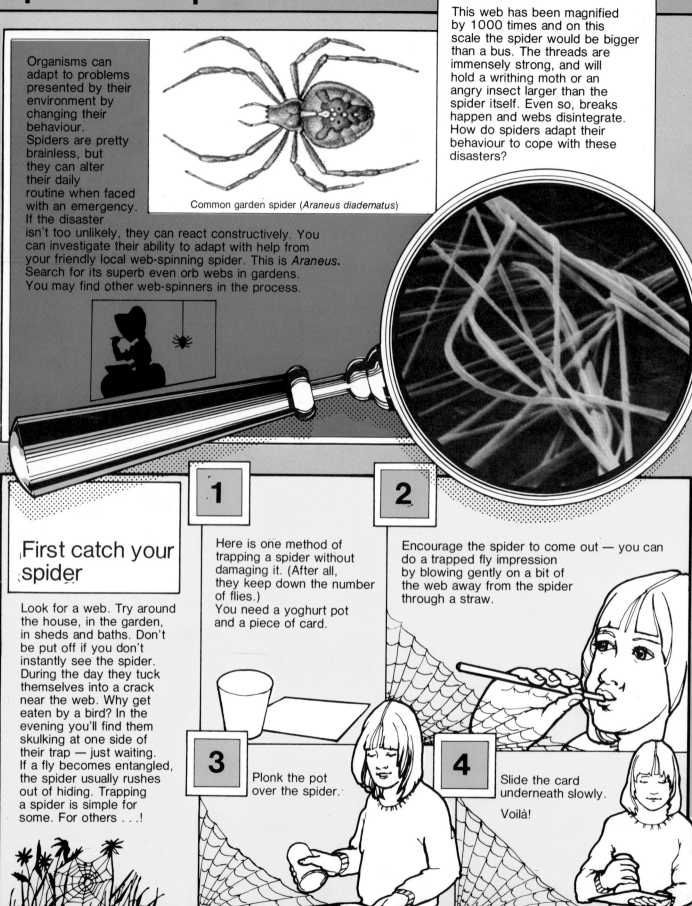

First catch your spider

Look for a web. Try around the house, in the garden, in sheds and baths. Don't be put off if you don't instantly see the spider. During the day they tuck themselves into a crack near the web. Why get eaten by a bird? In the evening you'll find them skulking at one side of their trap — just waiting. If a fly becomes entangled, the spider usually rushes out of hiding. Trapping a spider is simple for some. For others . . .!

1
Here is one method of trapping a spider without damaging it. (After all, they keep down the number of flies.)
You need a yoghurt pot and a piece of card.

2
Encourage the spider to come out — you can do a trapped fly impression by blowing gently on a bit of the web away from the spider through a straw.

3
Plonk the pot over the spider.

4
Slide the card underneath slowly.

Voilà!

Webs on twigs

Webs in boxes

You need

An old shoe box

A spider
A roll of cling-film

A piece of wire (to hang—my trusty clothes hanger)

You need

Bare twig (leaves get in the way)
Stable bottle or pot
Optional cover (glass mixing-bowl or an upside-down storage jar)

What to do

Spiders need hooks to hang their webs on — fit the wire into the box like this:

Persuade your spider that it really does want to go into the box

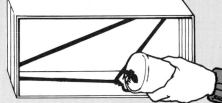

Cover the front of the box with a layer of cling-film

If it's evening and quiet, your spider may spin as you watch. Encourage it with a fly. Wind blows branches around. What does the spider do if you pull the box diagonally? How much twisting will the web take before it rips?

What to do

1 Place a leafless twig in a small plant pot

Introduce your spider to the twig

2 Given peace and evening-time it will spin a web. Try not to disturb it

4 Sometimes insects escape and tear a hole in the web in the process. Make a small hole (½cm / ¼in) across the web. What does the spider do?

3 What does the spider do if a small piece of twig 'accidentally' gets caught in the web?

5 Make larger holes. At what stage does the spider give up or start a new web?

On being a bit scientific

It's basic to know what a spider usually does before we start setting it problems. How does the spider know there is food in the web? (Hint — watch its front feet.) Does the spider react in the same way to small and large live prey; or raw meat and bits of lead out of a pencil?
Write down what you see in a notebook as you see it. Everyone always forgets details after a while.
P.S. Spiders are not passionately fond of living in boxes. Let yours go after a day or so and catch a new one.
One last thing. Your spider may stump around the edge of the web and appear to sulk. Probably it's frightened. It may turn out that the best way to do your experiments is with your spider comfortably at home on its own web in the garden (or shed).

Signs of the times

Date a fish

No, not that kind of date. You don't have to go for a swim off the Peruvian coast to learn something about the way fish grow. All you need is a fish (not deep-frozen blocks reputed to be fish) but real fish with scales. If it has head and tail all the better. Also take a look at the gills and inside the gut. If you are lucky you may find some parasitic worms making a living. (Wash your hands carefully afterwards.)

More date a fish

What to do

Look at some scales from your fish with a hand lens. When you find one with clear growth rings, do a sketch of it.

Fish scale actual size

Actual length
Length at age 4
Length at age 3
Length at age 2
Length at age 1
Age in years 1 2 3 4 5

Ring growth is often proportional to overall growth. If you have a whole fish, you can work out how long it was at the end of each year of its life.

This fish perhaps ate less well in later life but it's more likely it developed other interests. Eggs and sperm take lots of energy to produce!

Growth rings

Many organisms have bursts of growth — say in spring when there's food and warmth and life is good. A season's growth is recorded in a wide ring of hard material (wood, scales, shells). Each wide band is followed by a narrow band of material produced when growth is slow. Pine trees perched on mountain-sides always find life so tough they look very like Bonsai trees. Their growth rings are very narrow and close together. The cross-section (left) is of a Californian Bristle cone pine which has been a few

thousand years a'growing. Rings very close together show when growth was very slow, perhaps in particularly cold years. Take a rubbing of the trunk of a felled tree to record the growth history of your local trees.

Pitcher closed

Pitcher open

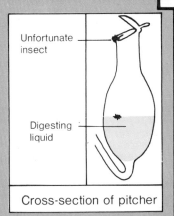

Unfortunate insect

Digesting liquid

Cross-section of pitcher

In places where recycling is slow, an ambitious plant out to make new tissues finds itself short of the vital element nitrogen in its usual form. Carnivorous plants have adapted to this limitation by trapping the element on the move — while it is part of a passing insect. The mechanisms vary. The pitcher plant from the sodden forests of Sarawak grows a leaf tube with a scree slope of slippery scales. There is a digesting pool at the bottom of the pit. When the lid opens, the trap attracts insects with a sweet scent. Once in, the victim cannot scramble out and drowns in the liquid which digests the corpse.

Take a trunk rubbing

You need

A wax crayon

Plain paper

Pins or nails to hold the paper in place

Make a fly trap happy

Venus fly traps and other carnivores are used to soggy environments. Bottle gardens suit them fine — this one is in a glass storage jar. Garden shops sometimes have insectivorous plants so why not grow a fly-eater yourself?

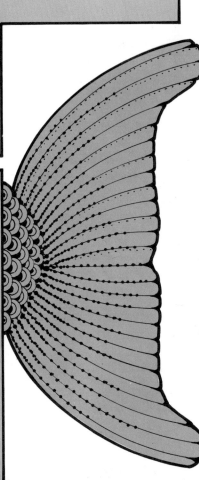

1 Fly trap

2 Sphagnum moss

3 Potting compost

4 Charcoal filter

5 Gravel

A fly trap has sensitive hairs on the inside of the leaves. Offer it a fly-sized bit of meat and trigger the leaf to close. Digestive fluids made by the plant will break down the meat so the leaf can absorb its nutrients.

Limiting growth

Why build a bonsai?

Bonsai trees show in their beautiful dramatic shapes the results of a severely limited growth. A plant's size can be reduced by lack of space, or warmth, by too much water, or by being eaten. When creating a bonsai, you are behaving like a very choosy rabbit, just nipping at the growing tips of roots and shoots. The tree is forced to grow only by the amount and in the directions you choose; you prevent it from doing anything else. Otherwise the mini-trees need soil and water and sunlight and conversation just like any other plant.

You can bonsai most trees if you catch them as seedlings. You might choose two of the same age and type; limit one and let the other grow as well it can in your garden as a comparison.

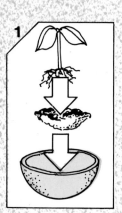

Bonsai is never very speedy, but you can see results faster if you grow your tree in half of an empty grapefruit.

1 Assemble your seedling, moist soil and grapefruit.
2 Sit the whole thing in a bowl and keep it moist but not sopping.

3 Every time a root tries to grow through the grapefruit skin, snip it off. Remove the stem tip bud too.

The slow way – roots

You need

Any seedling at the 2-leaf stage

A fair-sized flowerpot and a saucer

Gravel

Soil (or potting compost)

Scissors

What to do

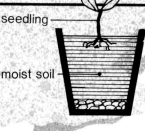

seedling

moist soil

Shake the soil off your seedling's roots. Chop off every single tip. Don't let the root dry out.

Repot.
Keep moist and in the shade till new leaves start. Then place it in the sun.
It will appreciate being left outside in mild weather.

At the end of the summer, shake the soil from the roots again. Prune all the tips again. Repot. Leave till next spring. Prune roots again. Repot in a shallow container. Prune roots every spring.

THE THEORY

Growing tips tend to be rather delicate and are easily damaged. Plants insure against this by having growing points further back on a shoot or root which will only grow if the tip is damaged. Chopping away at the tips tends to make the reserve buds grow. It is best to stick to trees because not all plants have their growing points in the same place — the giant kelp for example has growing points at both ends!

Bonsai trees can be trained into many shapes. It takes a long time but it is endlessly fascinating watching your tree grow.

Japanese flowering cherry

Bonsai pine trees

Trident maple about 40 years old

Japanese hornbeam

The slow way – shoots

Trim the shoots at the same time as the roots for a good tree shape. All you need is scissors.

What to do

1 Wait till your plant is a little taller than you really want it to be. Cut off the tip to just above the next bud down.

2 Remove all the leaves and buds you do not want to grow into side shoots.

This is an aerial photo of a field. The pale areas are where plants are growing poorly because ancient walls reduce their roots' growth – bonsai on the grand scale.

Buried wall reduces root growth

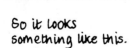

3 So it looks something like this.

4 Now the main tip has been removed, these will grow into this.

Now remove their tips and the buds and leaves you don't want to develop. And so on. By now the leaves your Bonsai is producing will be much smaller than its sister in the garden.

You and your limits

But I'm too stupid...

What are man's limits? Some of them are fairly straightforward. It's not easy to be in two places at once. You may well be too big, too small, too young, too old or too weak. Some limits change with time or effort; others won't. Make your own personal limitations list. What stops *you*?

We've all thought we're stupid at times — but what does it mean? Intelligence is hard to define. Partly it's what you use to solve problems. But there are a great many kinds of problems. Try these . . .

1

LIMITED
means the opposite of:

EDGED

UNRESTRICTED

CLEAR

ECOLOGICAL

FINITE

6 How many uses can you think of for a fishing net?

2

FERN

PINE TREE

ROSE BUSH

FUNGUS

OAK TREE

MOSS

Underline the one word which does not belong with the rest.

5 Which is the shape which goes next?

3 Fill in the + and − signs between these numbers so they give the right answer.

1 2 3 4 = 2

1 − 2 + 3 − 2 = 0

1 + 2 − 3 + 4

4 Which is the smallest fraction but one?

$$\frac{1}{3}$$

$$\frac{31}{36}$$

$$\frac{11}{12} \quad \frac{5}{6} \quad \frac{17}{18}$$

What matters here is not whether you can do them all, but which ones you find easy to do. The first two are about your ability with language, the next two are about number thinking. Visual think and creative thinking are only two of many other types of ability. Perhaps you can fix a bike, play an instrument or see which colours fit together well. It's important to remember your limits if you want to be a brain surgeon, but mostly it's better to hang on positively to your own potential — "I'm doing it because I'm good at/enjoy it." There is a school of thought that says pretty well anyone can learn pretty well anything, given enough time and patience.

ANSWERS

1 unrestricted

2 fungus (the rest are green)

3 1 + 2 + 3 − 4 = 2

4 $\frac{5}{6}$ (try putting them all over 36)

5

6 you can think of more than that.

It's interest that counts

People tend to do badly when they're not interested, and do well when they care. Assess yourself. In each group of activities in the list, choose the one you'd like to do most. Cover up the letters while you do it. At the end, add up your A's, B's and so on. Assume you can do anything you want.

Make a large glove puppet (like a Muppet)	D
Design an improved uniform for the Police	E
Have a job in the kitchen of a cafe	F
Work in a zoo feeding and caring for the animals . .	A
Help out at a handicapped children's playground . .	B
Be a dogsbody (filing, etc.) for a local newspaper .	C

Go to some lectures on using computers	A
Help organize a Christmas party at the youth club .	B
Catalogue and file photographs of past holidays . . .	C
Build a bird house and bird table	D
Act as photographer at a wedding	E
Go on a canoeing and camping trip	F

Keep a regular diary	C
Repair your bicycle	D
Learn to do batik (a dyeing technique)	E
Set up a rock garden	F
Design an intercom system between two rooms . .	A
Read to a blind neighbour	B

Enter a diving competition	F
Do a survey of colour blindness among your friends	A
Do the shopping for an elderly neighbour	B
Become treasurer for the local Charity Committee .	C
Redecorate your room at home	D
Write a short story	E

Make a collection of rock specimens	A
Be in the chorus of a musical	B
Plan, make and sell the tickets for a play	C
Set up the lights for a play	D
Design the sets and costumes for a play	E
Invent a safe but effective explosion for stage use .	F

What about "Oh it's not important for her — she's a girl," or "Boys don't cry"? Maybe you say, "Right and that's the way it ought to be." Maybe you grind your teeth and take it. Perhaps you'll change some of these limitations that the society you live in sets for you.

Make lists of things you can't do because other people stop you. Decide which are okay ("They won't let me drive a car until I'm . . . ") and which you could well do without. Which is the longer list? Do your family agree with your list? "I won't do it because I'm too cross, lazy, female, male, practising Buddhist, a vegetarian or haven't passed the right exams." I do this because I'm ambitious, female, male Catholic, black, white, happy, tense, in love or interested." Limited food supply or lack of shelter don't seem to trouble us much — at least not in developed countries. YET. Have you read *Make Room Make Room* by Harry Harrison or *Stand on Zanzibar* by John Brunner (both science fiction set in a crowded future)?

This is only a short test and so may not be very accurate. In any case most people enjoy a variety of activities. It's not so much your test result but whether you agree with it or not, and your reasons.

Mostly A's — you're interested in science

B's — in working with people

C's — go for clerical work

D's — practical, like doing things

E's — are artistic

and F's — like active, outdoor pursuits

The reclamation game

A walk around some derelict places that could be greener

The rules

On the board are squares with happenings in them. Before you begin, decide how many squares backwards (B) or forwards (A) you should move for each event on the trail. Imagine you are David Bellamy when you do this, and gauge how damaging or beneficial each event is. Fill in the spaces with pencilled numbers. The events have all happened somewhere (though not all together).

You need a counter each and a dice. Throw a six to start.

In the valley

Start here

Town needs more water. Authorities decide to flood valley. **B**

Water authorities decide to build a reservoir in next valley. **A**

Conservationists decide to fight. Talk to Press. **B**

Conservationists find rare alpine plant in valley. **A**

Authorities claim they can't assess the value of the plant against that of water. **B**

Months pass as inquiry gets held up. **B**

Local government representative takes up case. Inquiry starts. **A**

Campaign to plant trees and shrubs on tip starts — it'll look better and be more stable. **A**

Interested solicitor looks up laws on dumping dangerous wastes. **A**

On the refuse tip

Letters of complaint are ignored. **B**

Fires break out in local tipping area. **B**

New lake fished out by over-enthusiastic and unlicensed fishermen. **B**

FINISH— AREA STARTS TO LOOK MORE INTERESTING

White steaming crystals which are very acidic found. **B**

On the car tip

Authorities ignore complaint.

B ☐

Local school surveys tip and proposes a tree screen.

A ☐

Visitors to see rare alpine plants start to erode valley sides as they walk.

B ☐

Local residents complain about car tip to authorities. Claim it is dangerous.

A ☐

Find solitary wasps' nest in battery.

A ☐

Local Press supports scheme.

A ☐

Tree screen planted. Tipping is now controlled.

A ☐

In the quarry

Local authorities obtain government grant for land reclamation.

A ☐

'No money,' say quarry owners.

B ☐

Disused quarry, with crumbly sides, is unfenced.

B ☐

Community holds fund-raising events.

A ☐

Students doing environmental studies propose flooding the quarry for fishing and sailing.

A ☐

Child breaks leg in quarry.

B ☐

Refugees and visitors

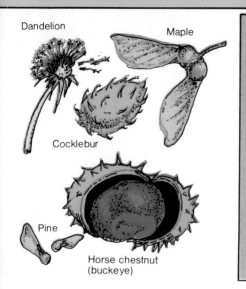

Dandelion

Maple

Cocklebur

Pine

Horse chestnut
(buckeye)

Your garden may be a more popular resort and refuge than you realise. Animals and plants are constantly on the move in search of new space and more food. Mostly you don't notice them.

Seed check

Carry out a seed check. Look for seeds in your turn-ups and shoe soles. How about your bicycle tyres or even your cat's fur? Working out who's who is done best by growing them. Reach for your trusty yoghurt pots (see p. 32); set up a nursery. Interesting-looking seedlings can be potted out later. You may get some surprises, but many will be familiar — dandelions and nettles have hitched lifts half-way round the world.

Model travellers

While sorting your heap of seeds you will probably find sticky or hooked seeds that have had a free ride. Other plants invest in wings or parachutes for their seeds. Design a winged seed and race it against a real one.

Thin card and scissors

Plasticine

Launching pad (or a chair)

Optional extra—a fan

What to do

Cut out your prototype wings

Affix a plasticine 'seed'- look at a real one for the correct proportions. Don't forget the seed includes a food supply for a young plant

Launch all seeds from the same height and with the same wind conditions

How can you improve your design?
Add a twist by pulling the card across the sharp edge of the scissors
Challenge the rest of your family to improve your design

Who wins?

Leaving tracks

Your garden has plenty of permanent residents but you probably have a number of visiting animals who come and go quietly — leaving their tracks behind if the ground is soft enough. You can check on these visitors even if you have rock-hard ground. People without a garden need not despair because window sills also have some interesting visitors. All you need is a track trap. Collect a shallow tray, powdered clay, water and a little bait. Mix the clay in water. You need a mix soft enough to take a print from a light animal but not runny enough that everything evens itself out. Then put the mix into the tray.

Put your tray out
Window sills are fine for birds

Bait the tray with a little food

Go away—and don't forget that no one of any interest will drop in to see you while you are only three feet away!

Lock up the cat...

Keeping a visitor's book
What to do — the easy bit

You need

A cardboard ring.
Vaseline.
Soft brush.
Liquid shellac or
   soft soap.
Plaster of Paris as
   thick as whipped
   cream — mix quickly
   and to reduce air
   bubbles, keep the
   spoon in your mix
   as you pour.
Water for mixing
   and cleaning.

Wash it gently to
get the last bits off

Let it dry slowly

1 Vaseline the inside of the tube

2 Place the tube over the print and push it into the ground or clay about ½ in.

3 Pour in Plaster of Paris.

6 Brush the soil off your cast – a 'negative' of the foot print

5 Lift cardboard and mould out and then separate the two

4 Let it set (it won't take long, but be patient)

You could stop now or carry on to:

The harder bit

1 Coat the interesting side with shellac or soft soap.

2 Put the cast back into the tube fun side up

3 Pour in fresh Plaster of Paris and let it set

4 Lift your mould or 'positive' foot print out. If the layer of shellac was evenly applied, it should come out easily.

Books will help you identify the tracks, though here are a few general ones.

Hints
Look for toe and pad number
Toe and pad arrangement
Are there claws?
What is the pattern of tracks?
How far apart are they?

Cat family

Rabbit types

Unshod pony

Deer family

Dog family

Mice

Squirrel family

Reclamation is possible

Out of the ice box

After a natural disaster like an Ice Age,
plants and animals move in to reclaim
devastated land. They need time, but they
do it. Vegetation started to move towards
the poles as the ice began retreating
20 000 years ago. Find your latitude on
this hemisphere to get an idea of how
the scenery outside your window has
changed since the end of the last
Ice Age. There are variations
if you are near the sea, mountains, etc.

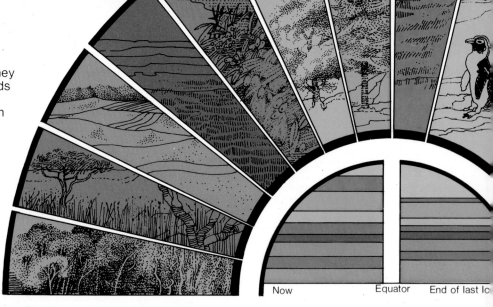

Monsoon | Savannah | Desert | Steppe | Mediterranean | Temperate | Boreal | Tundra | Ice

Now   Equator   End of last Ic

Living organisms can gradually turn
devastated land into a productive area
partly because they use material over
and over again. Man can create a
problem for this system if he takes
too much and replaces too little.
You've seen the holes in the ground
and scrubby wasteland and the heaps
of junk.

Groups of organisms are tough and
adaptable, but man goes far too fast
for them to keep up. In tropical
countries the plants have specialised
root and leaf systems to protect and
hold the soil in place. Replacing the
native plants with crops adapted to a
lower rainfall results, to man's
amazement, in everything being washed
away.

The art of pushing heaps into holes

You might think that the job of
tidying up mess belongs to those
who made the mess and the money
It rarely works out that way. The m•
could be dangerous holes or waste
dumped in heaps. The holes may be
in use and moving tips is expensive
Such legislation as exists may be
ignored. Play the reclamation game
for ideas on what to do. Involve
colleges and universities near you
— they may be interested in getting
a project going and helping you with
the authorities.

Warning

If you do decide to investigate
your area further remember that
quarries and tips can be dangerous
places. Every year a few people are
injured or killed in accidents in quarries.
Also they belong to someone. Ask before
you go scrambling around. Generally
people will give permission for
biological and geological
studies if a bit of ground
is no longer in
active use.

What can
be done about
this mess?

QUESTIONS TO SORT
OUT ARE:

Why has nothing
been done?

Could something
be done?

How best could it
be done?

Talk to people — not only will they
stop being faceless, they'll find it
much harder to say 'no' to you.

5 Trees

4 Shrubs

3 Scrubby grasses and weeds

2 Mosses

1 Lichens

Surveying the damage

Much can be done by watching and noting and drawing attention to change. Follow the changes in derelict land. A recently-abandoned tip is rather like a new island. It is a dry ocean, but the plants still arrive as seeds on birds' feet or by wind. Occupation proceeds in an orderly sequence unless disturbed. Lichens (**1**) are followed by mosses (**2**). Next to arrive are the scrubby grasses and weeds (**3**), then shrubs (**4**), and finally trees (**5**). This kind of steady replacement is known as a succession. All this takes many years.

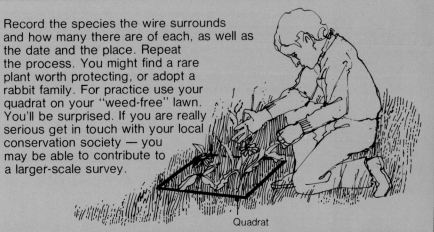

Tips with plant roots holding them together are much more stable than bare ones, and a tree planting scheme is usually a good idea. Follow progress with a survey which records the changes. The number of species present is important — the more the merrier. How many of each species gives an idea of how old the community is. You can't count the whole of your site so count in small squares of it. It can be investigated with tools like quadrats — which are simply bits of wire (old coathanger maybe) bent into a square and thrown randomly. Your sample lump of land is where it lands.

Record the species the wire surrounds and how many there are of each, as well as the date and the place. Repeat the process. You might find a rare plant worth protecting, or adopt a rabbit family. For practice use your quadrat on your "weed-free" lawn. You'll be surprised. If you are really serious get in touch with your local conservation society — you may be able to contribute to a larger-scale survey.

Quadrat

If you can't beat them — use them

If no-one can be persuaded to reclaim your quarry, it might still be full of fossils. If you are lucky and have good eyes you might find fossils shells standing out against rain-worn clay. Split shaley rocks may reveal a long-dead trilobite. Pebbles sometimes turn out to be sea urchins or ammonites.

You can get some idea of who they are from a good fossil book or the paleontology section of a museum. Serious collectors need a cold chisel, scrapers, enough bags and padding to individually wrap the specimens and a geological hammer. The hammer matters, as an ordinary one is liable to disintegrate when you hit rock. Leave buying a hammer until you're sure your local eyesore actually has some fossils in. Ask your library or local museum.

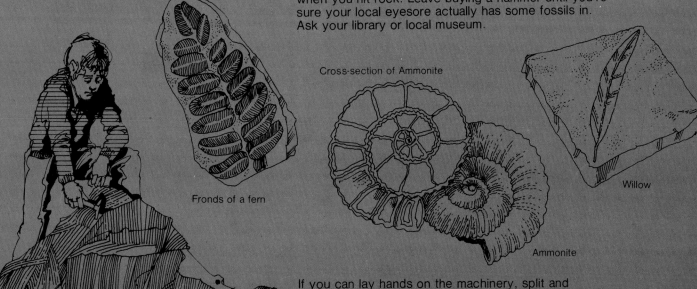

Fronds of a fern

Cross-section of Ammonite

Ammonite

Willow

If you can lay hands on the machinery, split and polish your fossils — they will look splendid.

The territory game

If you get up early you may well see the local birds sitting on their singing posts and letting rip. They are announcing to their relations that 'This bit of garden is mine'. In a world short of both safe places from cats and good food-hunting sites, many birds (and other animals) do their best to claim a territory of their own to breed and feed in. Having claimed it, they defend it from others interested in the same things. Tits, chickadees and honeysuckers (see p. 52) have opted to spread out a little and relatives use different parts of the environment.

Play the game to get the hang of what matters to territorial birds. You'll need two box dice (see p. 62) with the numbers 1 to 6 on one, and the letters A to F on the other, plus four area tokens each (use small sweets (candies) — winner eats half the tokens of the losers). Up to four birds can play.

The rules

You are a bird trying to capture a large enough area of land (four squares together) to raise a family on. You'll need to think about nesting sites and food. The map shows some back gardens which will do nicely, except that other birds (the rest of the players) are after the same things you are. You need to grab a patch and defend it. To occupy an area square you must throw a letter and a number.

In this case you would have square A4. Birds — sorry, players — take turns to throw. Once your four counters are on the board you continue to throw. If you get a better spot you can move any of your counters there.

If you throw the letter and number of a square someone else already has, don't hit them; be a civilized thrush and have a song contest — in this case cunningly disguised as a throw-off. The person who throws the highest number gets to keep the square.

Okay as territory patterns

Not okay as territory patterns

The game is over when half the players have got four squares together in a group.

Some squares are better from a bird's point of view than others. At the end of the game turn to page 63 for the scores for each square you possess. Those with four squares together can add four extra points. Highest score wins.

The squares have been rated on how valuable they are to a bird. If you think the scores aren't fair, there is a spare column on page 63 for your corrections. (Agree on them before you start playing.)

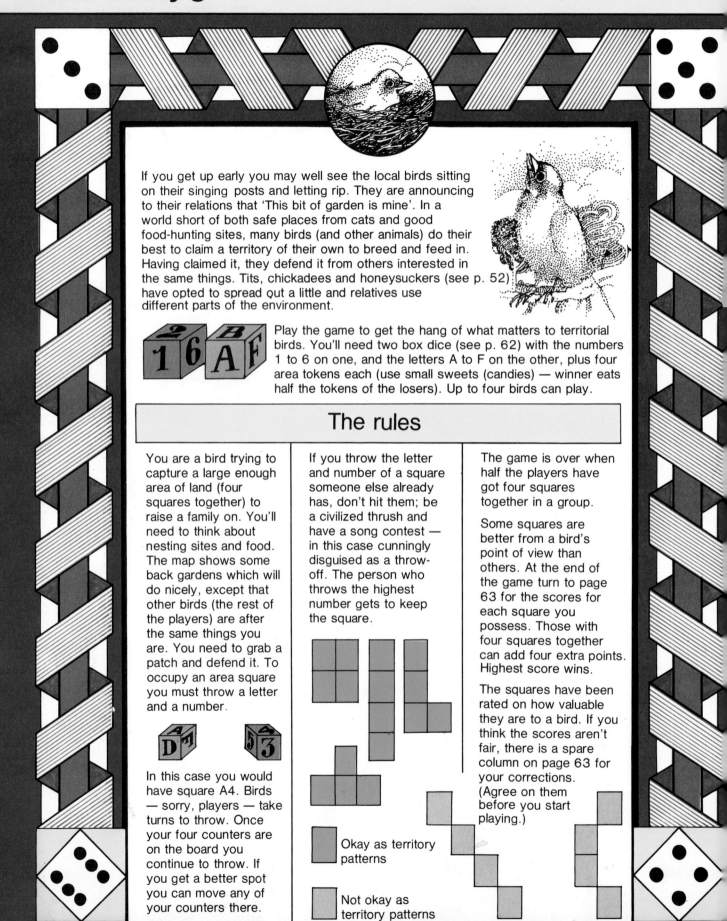

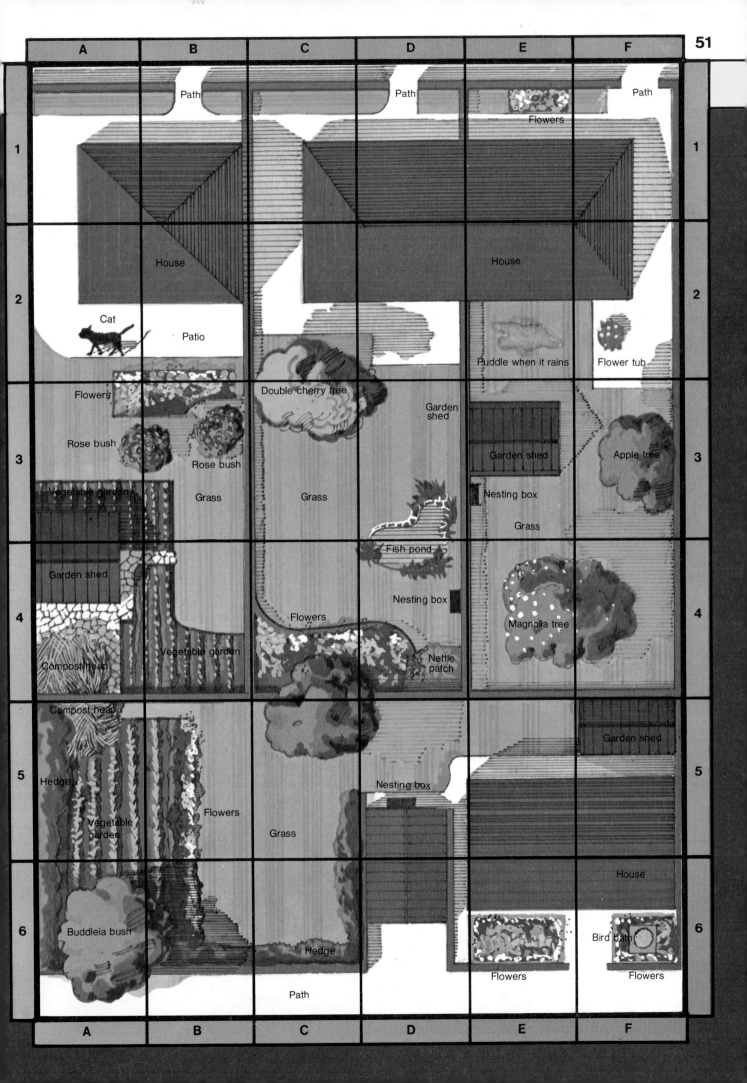

A · B · C · D · E · F

Path

Flowers

Path

Path

House

House

Cat

Patio

Puddle when it rains

Flower tub

Flowers

Double cherry tree

Garden shed

Rose bush

Rose bush

Garden shed

Apple tree

Vegetable garden

Grass

Grass

Nesting box

Grass

Garden shed

Fish pond

Flowers

Nesting box

Vegetable garden

Compost heap

Flowers

Nettle patch

Magnolia tree

Compost heap

Garden shed

Hedge

Nesting box

Vegetable garden

Flowers

Grass

House

Buddleia bush

Bird bath

Hedge

Flowers

Flowers

Path

Animal addresses

The Kestrel
Exits 16 — 17
M6 Motorway
CHESHIRE
England.

This kestrel is making a fair living by the edge of a motorway. He is after voles and other small mammals. If you wanted to write to this kestrel, his address would be ....

Why so much space? He needs many small animals to keep him going and they all need a home space. If he is to raise a family he and his mate will need an even larger territory, which must include a suitable place for a nest. Birds of prey spread themselves out to avoid over-hunting grass verges. On your next long trip, try writing the addresses of the ones you spot. How about:
Thorny Devil,
Near road at Andrewilla
Sturt's Stony Desert, Australia

A home is not enough

If you write out the addresses of some of your local animals, some will turn up in the same places. Don't they run out of food? The kestrel and the linnet have the same address but we could add kestrel (hunter) and linnet (shepherd's-purse collector). Add occupations to the addresses — it will sort your family out — what about other animals?

Name	Address	Occupation

A niche is a niche by any other name

Trendy ecology theory says that different groups of animals use different parts of the environment for feeding and breeding and generally living. Each bit is called a niche. Sometimes it takes a very close look to see that they are separate. Tits, chickadees and honeysuckers have all been closely studied. It turns out that when very closely related species live in the same tree, they use different bits of it. Mind you, few groups have been fully studied — there's room for fresh observations.

You can set up your garden or window sill or fire escape as a study centre — though be warned, this is an artificial situation. Birds may well feed differently left to themselves. Nevertheless, providing a variety of food, hung up at a variety of heights, should result in your having interesting visitors.

Bird watcher (binoculars are a helpful extra)

Birds won't be keen on a window sill, but you can try hanging offerings from a pole

Beech nuts on washing line

Bits of bacon

Ash

Berries

Coconut with smallish hole

Collect seeds in the autumn and hang them on branches later in the year

Frustrated cat

Pine branch with cones. Lots of birds recognise and like particular trees

Meal worms in a bowl

These are mixed seeds

Birds love a water supply

Keep up regular feeding if you want birds to know where you are.

Once upon a supercontinent

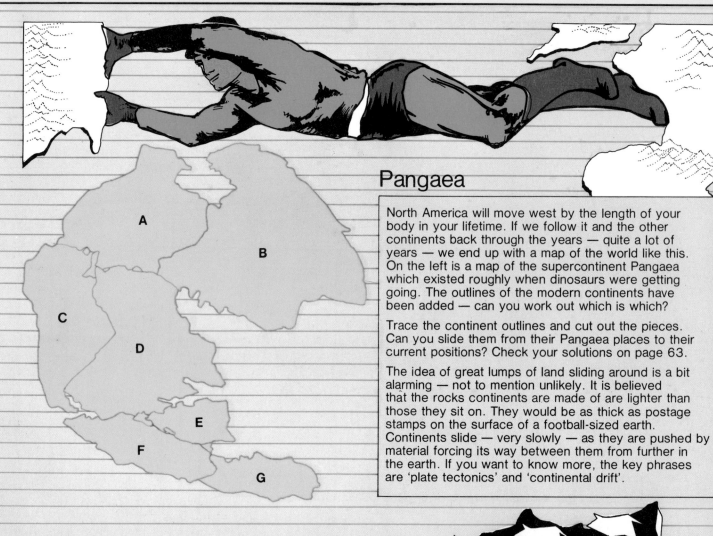

Pangaea

North America will move west by the length of your body in your lifetime. If we follow it and the other continents back through the years — quite a lot of years — we end up with a map of the world like this. On the left is a map of the supercontinent Pangaea which existed roughly when dinosaurs were getting going. The outlines of the modern continents have been added — can you work out which is which?

Trace the continent outlines and cut out the pieces. Can you slide them from their Pangaea places to their current positions? Check your solutions on page 63.

The idea of great lumps of land sliding around is a bit alarming — not to mention unlikely. It is believed that the rocks continents are made of are lighter than those they sit on. They would be as thick as postage stamps on the surface of a football-sized earth. Continents slide — very slowly — as they are pushed by material forcing its way between them from further in the earth. If you want to know more, the key phrases are 'plate tectonics' and 'continental drift'.

What happened to the continent's passengers?

Animals and plants have been moved around over the millions of years as their bits of land drifted around.

The imaginary continent (top) is occupied by equally imaginary Mugwumps. Black ones live in deserts, white ones in grasslands. In between the two main land masses are Mugwumps who are the result of patchy mating of the two kinds.

Over the years the two halves of the continent separate (bottom) and slide. Closely related Mugwumps are now geographically very far apart. What about today's world? Look at the map opposite.

The world today with clues

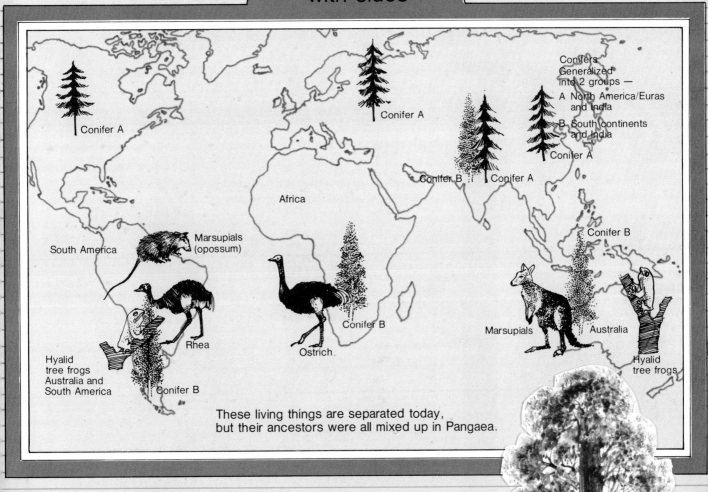

Conifer A

Conifer A

Conifers Generalized into 2 groups —
A North America/Euras and India
B South continents and India

Conifer A

Africa

Conifer B   Conifer A

Conifer B

Marsupials (opossum)

South America

Conifer B

Rhea

Marsupials   Australia

Ostrich.

Conifer B

Hyalid tree frogs Australia and South America

Conifer B

Hyalid tree frogs

These living things are separated today, but their ancestors were all mixed up in Pangaea.

Trace an ancestor

1 Diprodon was the largest ever marsupial — but where from?

2 Sequoia trees are only in the Western States of America today but guess where fossil sequoias have been found?

3 Kannemid reptiles from S. America — and where else?

4 Phororhacos stalked the plains — which ones were homes for this flightless bird?

5 Glossopteris once covered Africa — and which other places?

6 Paleoparadoxia — strange beasts. They left remains that turned up in the Western USA — and?

Make some educated guesses about these long-gone organisms. Bear in mind the way the continents were when they were part of Pangaea and the hints from the map above.

Man attacks defenceless environment!

People have a bad habit of pouring their wastes straight back into the environment. The Los Angeles smog is a spectacular example, but you will have your very own bit of pollution within walking distance. Your own definition of pollution may include smells, sights and strange floating objects you'd prefer to do without. How much of it could have been avoided? Have a prowl round your area and make a pollution map as the first step in doing something about it. Ways of measuring pollutants like dust are suggested on this page. Animals and plants by their presence, or more often their absence, can tell us a lot about pollution levels. The next few pages are about such living indicators.

Pollution map

You can draw an environmental map like this, or xerox an existing map (at your local library perhaps) and fill in your notes over it.

Water temperature 9°c. Found small fish, 3 water lice, 1 caddis fly larva, 4 freshwater shrimps and 3 sludge worms in sample.

Powdery green. Pleurococcus only in Calvin Park — no true lichens.

School

Marsh area. Birds nest in part of it, but a rubbish tip is taking over.

Local meteorological station (they're very helpful here)

Home. Dust rated medium — no lichen on local trees

XO Cement factory

Many young trees on this estate are already broken

Paint factory

Toy making factory. Very dusty

Library and museum

River Fleet

Power station

Busy noisy road — dust sample rated high

Water temperature 13°c. Sample included 12 sludge worms, 6 blood worms, 3 water lice.

Rubbish tip; soil acid compared to a sample from the park.

Sewage farm

What to do if you find pollution

Pollution builds up round you for all kinds of reasons from carelessness to sheer bloody-mindedness. Here are some things you might do: Write a polite hopeful letter to the factory or whoever you think the culprit is. Get someone to check your observations first (very important). Make it easy for them to back down.

1 January 1979

11 Penmo Upington,

James Rappaport M.P.
House of Commons
London SW1

Dear Sir,
I live in your constituency and would like to bring to your attention the pollution produced by the XO Cement Company. My friends and I did a survey of the River Fleet above and below this

Dust and noise

Noises that keep you awake at night need stopping. The kind that damage your ears are rarer but need more action. Some portable tape-recorders have a sound level meter which will give you a relative measure of noise around you. Smoke and dust tend to be generated by the same sources. Smoke is easily measured with a Ringleman chart — ask a conservation society about them. Some places are dustier than others. Using the method below you can compare different areas about you for dust.

Acid and alkali

If soil or water is very acid or alkali it can be a sign of pollution. Be warned — acid soils aren't always polluted. Pine trees make the soil around their roots acid and discourge competitors. Many industrial processes do produce wastes which affect the acidity of soil or water. Indicators change colour in the presence of an acid or an alkali. Universal indicator paper (if you can get it) will give you a measurement of acidity in pH. A pH of 7 is neutral; a pH from 6 down to 1 is acid; a pH of 8 and over is alkaline.

You can make your own indicator solutions using red cabbage; rose petals and black cherry will also work. A sample acid is lemon juice and a sample alkali is washing soda. Test your indicator with them before venturing out.

Making your own indicator

What to do

Get a handful of red cabbage leaves and tear them up.
Grind them in a food blender along with a little meths or water.
Pour off the liquid, but keep it. Throw away the leaves.
Use a little of liquid for each test.

P.S. The liquid doesn't keep very well so make fresh each time — and don't forget to carefully wash all the containers you have used.

Measuring dust

What to do

Make up some gelatine or jelly.

Pour it into saucers. You need only a shallow layer.

Let it set. Check the weather. Rain does strange things to jelly.

Put the saucers in safe places — it's no good if they get trodden on.

Keep one inside for comparison.

Leave them out for a day or two and then compare them.

Is it much dustier near the road?

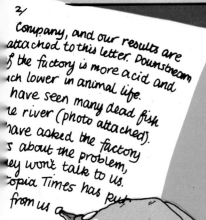

2/
Company, and our results are attached to this letter. Downstream of the factory is more acid and much lower in animal life.
have seen many dead fish the river (photo attached).
have asked the factory s about the problem, ey won't talk to us.
topia Times has put from us a

If the polluters won't talk — now is the moment for you to write to your local newspaper and local government. Include the local radio station too. Send them figures and photos. Talk to them yourself.

Still no joy? It's possible you have a case in law. This will be too much for you to handle, but conservation societies and government may be interested in taking up the case. Solid evidence is very important — good bets are dead fish, poisonous waste, excessive smoke and fumes, or dirt from a vehicle or factory.

UTOPIA TIMES
VICTORY FOR POLLUTION CAMPAIGN

Sensitive plants

Land plants, except triffids, have to grow where they start life. If man has made a real mess, they can't grow at all. If your sweet peas and zinnias refuse to co-operate it may be the pollution. They loathe the sulphur dioxide factories churn out. Some plants can act as a measure of pollution.

Lichen clues

Lichens are very touchy indeed about the amount of sulphur dioxide they can tolerate, and they make excellent pollution indicators. They keel over long before the levels of sulphur dioxide reach danger level for man and so act as a warning. They can be immensely tough and are often first and last plants into an area which has been cleared by ice or fire. Their problem is that they absorb a poison over all their surface. Small flat ones can cope with highish levels of pollution. Exotic feathery lichens with a huge surface area for their weight can only survive in truly clean air. Hunt for fragile types when you are trying to assess how polluted your home territory is. An area's pollution level is measured by the most sensitive you can find. The tougher types will co-exist with them. The lower on trees and walls your lichen grows, the more polluted the area. Finally, what if you can't find the more sensitive lichens but also can't see any factories? Could it be that you are to windward of an industrial area and sulphur dioxide is being blown in your direction? This would explain your scaly flat lichens and the lack of shrubby ones.

Very polluted . . . . Very clean

Zone 0 No lichens at all — powdery green algae at best. *Pleurococcus* is as tough as old boots.

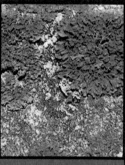

Zone 2 *Xanthoria* lichens, but only on stone, concrete, etc.

Zone 4 Even more leafy lichens. Surface area increases as air gets cleaner.

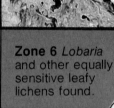

Zone 6 *Lobaria* and other equally sensitive leafy lichens found.

Zone 1 Crusty *Lecanora* lichen — like crazy paving.

Zone 3 Leafy *Parmelia* lichen found on tree trunks — orange *Xanthoria* found on trees too.

Zone 5 Shrubby lichens such as *Evernia*. Half the sulphur dioxide level of zone 2.

Checking the effect of a new factory

An area changes as new industries grow up. A before-and-after record is important, if you want to protest. Lichens are good evidence because they react very rapidly to new pollutants. Make a map of the way they grow before a new factory starts working.

| You need | A sheet of clear plastic | A waterproof marker pen | A book with lichen identification (like this one) |

| What to do | Choose a group of the most sensitive lichens in your area | Lay your plastic sheet over the lichen and without pressing too hard, draw the out line of the patches on your sheet | Date and label the sheet - species' name and place - keep it safe. Use it to check how things are going the same time next year. If the lichen population has been wiped out, it's worth investigating the matter further and keeping records. |

Plant dyes

It would be great to suggest you use lichens, as people once did, for dyeing. Too bad that in most places we've given them such a hammering that lichen colours MUST be out. You can try a version of an old technique with other plants — alder catkins and young bracken will give you greens; golden rod and heather flowers for yellow; browns from acorn cups, oak bark and walnuts; and purple from bilberries. There are many more. Some flower dyes fade attractively.

You need

A second-best pan and a largish spoon

Half a pair of tights

White cloth and a handful of dye plant

What to do

Put the thing to be dyed into the tights. (or should that be 'tight'?)

Put tights and dye material into the pan and top-up with water

Bring to the boil

P.S.

You may get colours that are very different from the plants you started with. Keep boiling until it looks right— with bark it may take some time.
Rinse once in hot water and once in cold.

Animal indicators

Some animals are particularly sensitive to polluted water and register their disapproval by dying or leaving. The tough ones are often found in relatively clean water as well as polluted areas. The animals opposite are sometimes used as clues to the state of water, although if you go out with a net, you'll catch many others — snails, flatworms and small fish among them. Counting how many kinds of animal you find can be revealing, as the rule is:

CLEAN WATER	DIRTY WATER
Many kinds of animal	Fewer kinds. Often with red blood to absorb oxygen from the depleted supplies available.

Collect water above and below factory outlets. Many factories return water, which they have used in cooling processes, to the river. This water is warmer than the rest and may affect the organisms living there. It is worth taking a thermometer. What is the effect of water which has run-off from farmers' fields — perhaps it contains dissolved artificial fertilizers? Is there a busy road near your stretch of water? Rain falling on the road and running down into your stream or lake can have all sorts of dissolved chemicals in it. Do your counts on the bank and tip your sample back in at the end of the day.

1 *Dugesia* (flatworm)
2 *Bithynia* (no common name)
3 *Asellus* (water louse)
4 *Viviparus* (river snail)

Sampling kit

Rubber boots. A good mare – also in boots – to pull you out when you fall in

A notebook – animals won't spread out evenly, so take 2 or 3 different samples

Date	
Place	
Map ref	
Last rain	
Animal name	

A pencil

A net

Hand lens

Shallow dish or tray to tip sample into

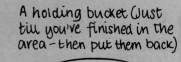

A holding bucket (just till you've finished in the area – then put them back)

The net

You need

25cm x 25cm square of fine mesh material (e.g. tights or so forth)
Wire (ex coat-hanger?)
Cane for handle
String

1 Weave the wire through the mesh

2 Bend the coat-hanger (or whatever wire you have) into a circle

Daphnia as water-testers

Daphnia and other water fleas are found in all kinds of water — they travel as eggs on birds' feet. These are happy daphnia swimming in their usual jerky way.

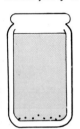

These are less happy daphnia in a sample of polluted water. RIP.

Daphnia much magnified

The water flea is usually transparent. If yours are red it means there is little oxygen in the water and the fleas are trying to compensate. Daphnia is the commonest water flea, but its many relatives also make good test animals.

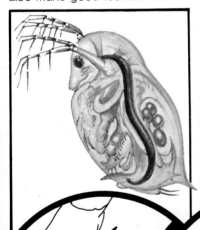

3 Twist the ends of the wire together tightly

4 Twist the wire around the cane and fix it firmly with string

A Clean water

MAYFLY NYMPH

A swimmer.
3 tails.
6 legs.
Lots of gills.

STONE-FLY NYMPH

A crawler.
2 long tails.
6 legs.

B Slight pollution

FRESHWATER SHRIMP

A swimmer.
Lots of legs.
Flattened body (sideways).

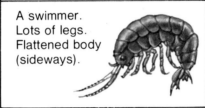

CADDIS-FLY LARVA

A crawler.
Lives in a case of stones, twigs, shells, plants or sand. May have a brightly-coloured head.

C Bad pollution

WATER LOUSE

A crawler.
Flattened body.
Many legs.

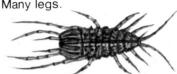

BLOODWORM

Fast swimmer.
Bright red.
Has false legs at each end.
Stumpy shape.
Has bunch of gills at one end.

D Very bad pollution

SLUDGEWORM

Long, thin. Tapering. Soft. Reddish.

RAT-TAILED MAGGOT

Not red but has a breathing tube to the surface.

Water where you live

One rainy day, draw a map showing water ways in your area and plot your results. A large coloured map with pictures of your animals looks great on a wall — especially if it's covered with a protective transparent film. Several years' worth of maps will show the effects of new factories and other changes on the level of water pollution.

Answers and information

Dice boxes

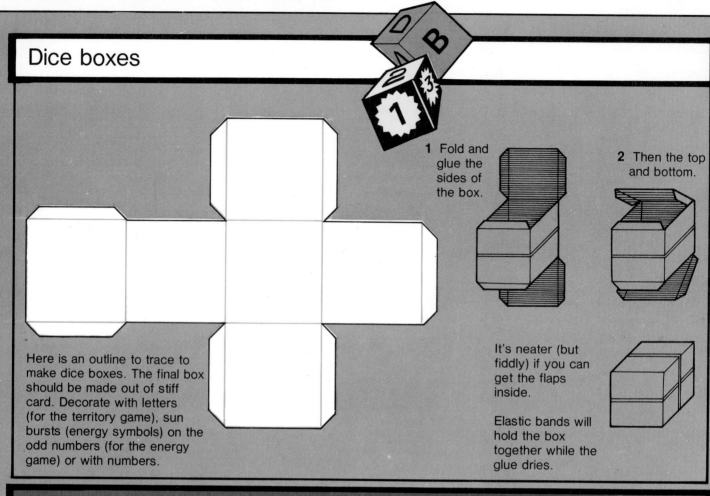

Here is an outline to trace to make dice boxes. The final box should be made out of stiff card. Decorate with letters (for the territory game), sun bursts (energy symbols) on the odd numbers (for the energy game) or with numbers.

1 Fold and glue the sides of the box.

2 Then the top and bottom.

It's neater (but fiddly) if you can get the flaps inside.

Elastic bands will hold the box together while the glue dries.

Checklist for the food chain game (page 22)

Top carnivores		Heron	Owl	Man	Titmouse	Pike
4	Eaten by	Man once thought them a delicacy — happily no longer.				Young might be eaten by a heron.

Intermediate carnivores		Adult trout	Spider	Cyclops	Predatory beetle	Frog	Thrush
3	Eaten by	Heron Man Pike	Frog Titmouse	Trout	Frog Spider Owl Titmouse	Heron Owl Pike	

Herbivores		Caterpillar	Land snail	Daphnia	Mouse	Water snail	Leaf-eating fly	Small fish
2	Eaten by	Titmouse Predatory beetle Spider	Thrush Titmouse	Trout Cyclops	Owl	Trout Heron	Spider Frog Predatory beetle Titmouse	Trout Man Heron Pike

Plants		Moss	Grass	Nettle	Oak tree	Algae	Wheat	Algae	Water-weed
1	Eaten by	Caterpillar Fly Snail	Caterpillar Fly Mouse	Fly Caterpillar Man	Fly Caterpillar	Daphnia Water snail Small fish	Caterpillar Fly Man Mouse	Daphnia Water snail Small fish	Daphnia Small fish

Incidentally, "On Ilkley Moor baht'At" doesn't mention the plants on Level 1 at all. For shame.

Checklist for the territory game (page 50)

You are occupying 4 squares. Look each up and add up your score. For your next game, rather than memorise the numbers, think harder about what makes a place valuable to a bird. You might even want to change the scores — use the spare column.

Box			Score		Reason
A1 D1	B1 B2	C1	1		Mostly house (you nest in trees and hedges). Besides, house in A has a cat.
E1	F1	B5	2		Flower-bed to attract insects. Long way from cat.
A2			2		That cat.
D2	F4	E5	2		Nothing special.
C2	E2		3		Flowering trees attract food. Good for insects.
A3	B4		4		Bit close to cat, but near shed and vegetable garden.
F6			4		Near the edge but useful water supply.
F5 F2	F3	E6	4		Nice trees and flowers. Bit near path.
B3			5		Rotten cat but shrubs to hide and flowers and vegetables.
C3			5		Water supply and cherry tree.

Box			Score		Reason
C5	D6		4		Nothing special but sheltered and good position.
D3			6		Water supply. Place near nest.
C6	D5	E3	5		Okay. Near nest box and shed.
A4			6		Cat but places to hide. Vegetable garden gets dug over. Also compost heap.
C4			7		Water and food, especially nettle patch which attracts butterflies.
E4			7		Tree nesting. Insects in spring. Shelter.
A5			8		Compost heap etc. as food. Sun. Hedge shelter.
B6			9		Buddlea great for insects. Shelter.
A6			10		Buddlea for insects. Shelter. Water.
D4			10		Food, water, and a place to breed. Great.

Once there was a supercontinent (page 56) — answers

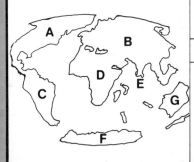

Map letters mean:
A N. America
B Asia
C S. America
D Africa
E India
F Antarctica
G Australia

Ancestors

1 Diprotodon lived in Australia.
2 Sequoias were found in Europe, Asia and all North America.
3 Kannemid reptiles also lived in Africa.
4 Phororhacos lived in South America.
5 Glossopteris lived in Africa, Australia, South America, India and Antarctica.
6 Paleoparadoxia also lived in Japan.

Botanic Action Kit - special offer

The Artemia described on pages 8 and 9 and the Gro-Kit illustrated on page 16 are available in a special Botanic Action Kit which is available only to Botanic Action readers.

The Artemia come in a sachet containing eggs and food. Add the contents to water and you will soon have some unusual and interesting pets.

The Gro-Kit has been manufactured by Fisons. It contains four miniature bags of growing medium with seeds and a capillary watering mat. All you need to do is open the bags and ensure that they are kept moist. As the seedlings grow, you will be able to see the effect of various mineral salt deficiencies. It will be your own tiny experimental garden.

The address to write to for the kit is:
AQUASCIENCE U.K.,
Dept. BMO
7 Cherry Blossom Lane,
Cold Norton,
Chelmsford,
Essex CM3 6JQ,
England.

UK orders should be accompanied by a cheque or postal order for £1·50 payable to Aquascience UK, plus 20p postage and packing. Overseas orders will be supplied — details are available on application to the above address. The price of the kit will hold until December 1980 but the offer is subject to availability.

The Green Earth

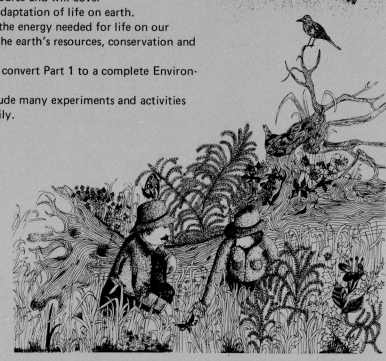

The National Extension College are offering a home-study course in Ecology/Environmental studies to adults who want to take the concepts of Ecology further. The course will be published in two parts.

Part 1 will stand on its own as a short-study course and will cover many exciting topics, tracing the evolution and adaptation of life on earth. The course is called "The Green Earth" because the energy needed for life on our planet comes from plants. We will also examine the earth's resources, conservation and pollution.

Part 2 will cover the extra topics necessary to convert Part 1 to a complete Environmental Studies O level.

Both parts are extensively illustrated and include many experiments and activities to do on your own or with your friends and family.

National Extension College

131 Hills Road
Cambridge CB2 1PD
Telephone 0223-63465

Photograph Acknowledgements

1	Mary Crewe	32	M.J.D. Hirons
4	Graham Morris	36	Picture produced by Kodak Park Industrial Laboratory, Eastman Kodak Company
7	Mike Ballentyne/M.J.D. Hirons/Michael Feldman	38	Mike Ballentyne
12	Professor Donald Lee	39	Graham Morris
16	The Tea Board of India/Fisons Ltd.	41	West Air Photography, Weston-super-Mare
18	M.J.D. Hirons	44	Michael Wright
19	D.J. Bellamy	58	Philip Harris Biological Limited
20	Primrose Hill Books	60	Michael Wright
25	Tesco Ltd.		Cover photograph: Michael Wright
28/29	Michael Wright		